Secure Your Legacy:
Estate Planning & Elder Law for Today's American Family

By Richard J. Shapiro, J.D., CELA, CAP

*For Terri, Emily, and Aaron,
who inspire me every day*

Table of Contents

Table of Contents i

Acknowledgments iii

Preface iv

PART I: ESTATE PLANNING BASICS 1

   Chapter 1 - Why Do I Need to Have an Estate Plan? 2

   Chapter 2 - Common Estate Planning Myths 27

   Chapter 3 - Funding & Maintenance: The Glue to an Effective Estate Plan 49

PART II: CUSTOMIZING YOUR ESTATE PLAN 57

   Chapter 4 - Estate Planning for Blended Families 58

   Chapter 5 - Planning For Loved Ones With Special Needs 61

   Chapter 6 - Estate Planning for Unmarried Couples 67

   Chapter 7 - Estate Planning For the Family Business 70

   Chapter 8 - Estate Planning For Retirement Assets 73

   Chapter 9 - More Specialty Planning Topics 81

PART III: ESTATE & GIFT TAXES 89

   Chapter 10 - The Skinny on Estate Taxes 90

   Chapter 11 - Gift Taxes & the Effective Use of Gifts 96

PART IV: ASSET PROTECTION - LIFE INSURANCE & MORE 102

   Chapter 12 - Integrating Life Insurance With Your Estate Plan 103

   Chapter 13 - Basic Asset Protection Strategies 112

PART V: PLANNING FOR DISABILITY - LONG-TERM CARE & MEDICAID PLANNING 118

Chapter 14 - The Importance of Planning for Incapacity 119

Chapter 15 - Proactive Planning for Long-Term Care: The Medicaid Asset Protection Trust 125

Chapter 16 - Long-Term Care: How Will I Pay the Cost? 133

Chapter 17 - Medicaid For Long-Term Care 138

PART VI: ADVANCED PLANNING STRATEGIES 186

Chapter 18 - Charitable Giving 101 187

Chapter 19 - QTIP Trusts 192

Chapter 20 - Qualified Personal Residence Trusts 195

Chapter 21 - Domestic & Offshore Asset Protection Trusts 198

Chapter 22 - Sales to Intentionally Defective Grantor Trusts 201

PART VII: ESTATE SETTLEMENT & BEYOND 204

Chapter 23 - Settling an Estate 205

Chapter 24 - Counseling: The Key To An Effective Estate Plan 218

Appendix A 221

INDEX 224

Acknowledgments

Forging a successful career requires the support of many people, and I am blessed to have a wonderful family and a great team at my law firm. My wife, Terri, and children, Emily and Aaron, are a source of endless love and inspiration. My colleagues and staff at Blustein, Shapiro, Frank & Barone, LLP have provided me with a platform to hone my skills and craft for over 20 years, and I especially thank my past and current partners Michael Blustein, Tad Barone, Will Frank, Jay Myrow, Rita Rich, Diana Puglisi, and Megan Conroy for giving me the freedom to build an estate planning and elder law department that is second to none.

I have had wonderful mentors since being admitted to the bar more than three decades ago. Burt Blustein, who recently passed away, provided sage guidance for building and managing a law firm, and was one of the most outstanding attorneys we have seen in the Hudson Valley. And my father, Art Shapiro, inspired me to follow in his footsteps to go into the law. I was lucky to practice with him for a decade, and he taught me to go above and beyond in service to my clients. He showed me the good lawyers can do for society, and I am forever grateful for the example he set.

My late mother, Harriet, also instilled in me a love of the English language that has helped my writing throughout my career.

Kudos too to my phenomenal estate planning and elder law team, including attorney Megan Conroy, recent law school graduate Mehvish Maqbool, and our assistants, Donna Wood, Lauren Dillon, and Sara Bennaci, who are unfailingly patient and are so vital to our success.

Preface

When this book was first published in 2017, it fulfilled my long-desired goal of providing the public with an easy-to-read resource for understanding the most common issues in estate planning and elder law. These topics can be complicated, and all too often people rely on what I call "Marge from the coffee shop" advice in making what can be life-altering decisions about how to plan their estate and protect their assets.

Much has changed in the world of estate planning and elder law in the five years since the first edition was released. This revised edition provides up-to-date information about new laws and new planning strategies and incorporates some new topics that were not included in the prior edition. This revised edition also includes the current (as of 2022) estate and gift tax exemption amounts; a review of the "SECURE Act", which has changed the landscape of planning with retirement assets; and other legal updates, including a major reboot of New York's statutory Power of Attorney statute.

While I am licensed to practice in both New York and Pennsylvania and am on "inactive" status with the District of Columbia Bar, most of my clients and cases are based in New York. While I have attempted to often integrate national perspectives in describing the various issues described in the book, readers will note that most examples and cases cited are based on New York law, and I make no assurance that the information will apply in every jurisdiction. And, being the dutiful lawyer I am, here is this routine disclaimer: *The information in this book is for general information only and is not, nor is it intended to be, legal advice.*

As you go through the chapters, a continuous theme will become readily apparent: creating a successful estate plan doesn't happen by luck but requires the involvement of a well-qualified estate planning attorney.

There will be both a time and financial commitment to doing it right, but isn't your family—and preserving your legacy—worth it?

Richard J. Shapiro, J.D., CELA, CAP
July 2022

PART I: ESTATE PLANNING BASICS

Chapter 1 - Why Do I Need to Have an Estate Plan?

Estate Planning Fundamentals

Many people erroneously believe that tax avoidance is the only reason to do estate planning, and therefore only the "wealthy" need to establish an estate plan beyond a basic *last will and testament*. But even for people of more modest means, **a well-conceived estate plan is a must**. Estate planning is more than just tax planning. Estate planning allows you to:

- Plan for your own mental incapacity so you need not rely on the courts to choose who will take care of you and your needs if you cannot manage your personal and financial affairs.

- Designate those persons who will make health care decisions for you upon your incapacity.

- Set your own preferences for life-support procedures.

- Retain control of how your assets are distributed upon your death.

- Ensure that your assets are protected if you need long-term care.

In short, through various estate planning tools, you can ensure that your assets will go to your chosen beneficiaries *when you want* and *the way you want*.

But too often the planning professionals hinder effective estate planning. If you put an estate planning attorney, CPA, life insurance agent, and financial advisor in one room, what issue do you think they are most likely to discuss? If you said taxes, you are probably right. As professionals, our training leads us to explore the most complex and challenging aspects of our respective fields. Given the complexity of our tax system, and the significant depletion taxes can cause to a family's assets, it's no surprise that estate planning professionals devote so much time and effort to learn the latest tax-saving strategies.

Unfortunately, this tax-centric focus often leads to the conclusion that the success of an estate plan is determined solely by the inclusion of estate-tax reduction language. Too often, such a narrow focus obscures the real reasons clients are seeking assistance, which is to provide for personal planning goals beyond mere tax planning.

During the counseling process, we must have a thorough understanding of the other family members and the **overall family dynamics**. Each family has its own quirks and issues, and it is essential that the client, as the expert on family matters, educates the estate planning attorney about the family situation. Once the attorney has gained a thorough understanding of the family picture, he or she can then teach the client about the estate planning techniques and the law most applicable to that client's situation. Only by combining these different sources of expertise can the client and attorney *together* create a customized estate plan suitable for that client's needs.

After understanding the family's particular dynamics and needs, we can then focus on the **client's wealth**. Experience shows us that our clients want to first preserve and protect their accumulated wealth, and then they wish to look at ways to enhance their wealth.

Finally, we address the strategies and tools to **save taxes and administrative expenses**. Like the last piece of a puzzle, this is the easiest piece to complete—but only if all the appropriate groundwork has been laid.

By focusing first on the family's personal planning goals and concerns—issues which, in "traditional" estate planning, are often relegated to the back burner—we can create an estate plan that is family-centric, as opposed to tax-centric. It's not a case of ignoring tax planning; rather, tax planning needs should be properly evaluated **only after** the planning fundamentals are addressed.

Intestacy: Allowing the State to Create Your Estate Plan

There is a common belief that if a person does not execute a will, then "everything will go to the state." While it is rare that the assets of someone who does no planning actually passes to the state, in failing to complete a formal estate plan, that person is permitting the state to effectively draft the person's estate plan.

If a person dies without an estate plan and owns assets in his or her name only—which does *not* include retirement plan assets, life insurance, and "POD" bank accounts[1] payable to named beneficiaries—then the person is said to have died *intestate*. Under New York law, for example, if the deceased person (the "decedent") has probate assets, those assets will pass to the decedent's survivors as follows:

- If there is a surviving spouse and "issue" (i.e., children or the children of any predeceased children), the spouse receives the first $50,000, plus one-half of the remainder, with the balance to pass to the issue "by representation." For example, if there is one living child and a deceased child who is survived by two of his own children (i.e., the decedent's grandchildren), the living child takes one-quarter

---

[1] The terms POD, TOD, and ITF all refer to a form of ownership that ensures that assets titled with one of those designations will pass to one or more named beneficiaries upon the asset owner's death by operation of law.

of the remainder, and the two grandchildren each take one-eighth of the remainder.

- If there is a spouse and no issue, the spouse receives the entire probate estate.

- If there is issue and no spouse, then the entire probate estate passes to the issue, by representation.

- If there is no spouse or issue, but one or both parents are living, then the entire probate estate passes to the surviving parent or parents.

- If there are siblings but no spouse, issue, or parents of the decedent, then the whole passes to the siblings, by representation.

The statute provides for additional, and rarely used, scenarios for distributions to grandparents and more distant relations.

By allowing the statutory provisions to govern, a person may create a nightmare for his or her family. For example, most married clients want his or her surviving spouse to benefit from the couple's entire estate, with the assets of the first spouse to die to be distributed either outright to the survivor or held in some form of trust. However, the children will receive approximately 50 percent of the deceased parent's individually owned assets. Not only will the spouse often be left with insufficient assets on which to live, but this disposition can be especially troublesome where a child is a minor or disabled beneficiary. In such a case, a court will typically appoint a *guardian ad litem* to represent the child's interests. Under New York law, the court will direct where the child's share of the inheritance will be held, decide how it is to be invested (almost always conservatively), and impose other limitations. The minor child will also be provided access to the remaining funds upon reaching majority age (typically 18 years old). Most people cringe thinking about allowing their 18-year-old children full control and access over their inheritance!

The rules of intestacy can also play havoc with Medicaid eligibility where a person in need of long-term care unexpectedly inherits assets. A few years ago, an 84-year-old man, "Joe," came to see me with one of his two surviving sons, "Gabe." Joe has another son, "Alan," and had a third son, "Ben." Ben died suddenly of a heart attack at 48 only a few months before our meeting.

For a few years prior to Ben's death, Joe had been dealing with several health issues, including diabetes and memory loss, and he had poor balance and was susceptible to falling. Joe had been residing part of the time with Ben at Ben's home in the Bronx, and with Gabe, who lives in Orange County, New York. By the time of our meeting, Joe's condition had deteriorated to where he could not be left alone, and his sons were seeking in-home caregivers for their father.

Joe was getting by on Social Security and a small pension, and because his resources were below the applicable Medicaid resource allowance, he would have been immediately eligible for Community Medicaid services. But when the unthinkable happened and Ben died at such a young age, the dynamics changed.

Ben's premature death, which was tragic enough, resulted in even more complications for Joe and his family. Ben's estate, estimated at about $1.1 million, consisted of his Bronx two-family residence, his "country" home in Orange County, and about $400,000 held in bank accounts. Because Ben, who was not married and had no children, died without a will, he died *intestate*. Therefore, his estate was distributed as provided under New York's intestacy statute, Section 4-1.1 of the Estates, Powers, and Trusts Law.

Under the intestacy statute, since Ben died unmarried and without descendants, Ben's entire estate passed to Joe as his surviving parent. Upon receipt of Ben's assets, Joe was no longer automatically eligible for Community Medicaid services. To retain eligibility for Community Medicaid, Joe had to transfer the newly inherited assets either to his surviving sons, or, preferably, to a Medicaid Asset Protection Trust. Since there are presently no resource transfer penalties for Community Medicaid eligibility in New York, after transferring the inherited assets to his surviving sons or a Medicaid Asset Protection Trust, Joe remained immediately eligible for Community Medicaid services.

The potential problem with that scenario, however, was that Joe's transfer of the inherited assets to either his sons or a trust *will* cause the imposition of a Medicaid transfer penalty should Joe require nursing home care within five years of the asset transfers. Given his rapidly declining health at the time of our meeting, that was a real possibility. Therefore, the transfer of Joe's assets to retain Community Medicaid eligibility had to be well-planned so that some or all the assets could have been returned to Joe should he need nursing home care within five years after the asset transfer. Under that scenario, Joe could still engage in "half-a-loaf" planning that can preserve 50 percent or more of the assets of a nursing home Medicaid applicant.

This complicated scenario could have been avoided, however, had Ben executed even a "simple" will that directed for the disposition of his assets to his brothers or other beneficiaries, presumably not including his father.

It is understandable why 48-year-old unmarried men with no children would think meeting with an attorney to do estate planning might not be that important. But as this real-life story of Joe and his sons demonstrates, if people do not arrange their affairs during their lifetime, the state will "design" their estate plan, and the results may not be pretty!

Doing no estate planning takes control of your affairs away from you and your family and turns it over to the "system," including lawyers, judges, clerks, and other well-meaning people who are nonetheless constrained by the law, regardless of your intentions or how the law might affect your survivors. **Make sure that *you* retain control of your affairs by attending to your planning needs.**

What Is Probate, and Why Do I Want to Avoid It?

Clients often seek a lawyer because of a desire to "avoid probate." Sometimes a client has been through a drawn-out probate administration for a parent or other relative that has left him or her frustrated. But often clients cannot tell me a reason why this is an important objective, only that he or she has heard that probate is "bad."

Probate is the legal process whereby a deceased person's individually owned assets must be administered before they can be distributed to the decedent's beneficiaries. If the decedent had a valid will, the assets would pass to the beneficiaries named in the will. As described in the previous section, if the person did not have a valid will, then the person is deemed to have died "intestate." In which case, the intestacy laws of the state where the person was domiciled at the date of death will determine the disposition of the person's assets.

If all the family members cooperate, a simple probate can be completed in a matter of weeks. More commonly, however, a probate estate will be completed from three months to well over a year (for more complex estates).

The horror stories arise typically where a beneficiary challenges either the validity of the will itself or the manner that the estate is being administered by the executor or administrator. In contested estates, the proceeding may last for many years, with legal and accounting fees totally well into the tens or even hundreds of thousands of dollars.

Most problems attributed to probate are not endemic to the legal system itself; rather, these "out-of-control" estates are more likely the result of poorly conceived or executed estate planning—or the failure of the decedent to do planning in the first place.

Because of the common aversion to probate, people are often convinced to do anything and everything to avoid a probate proceeding. However, the cure is often worse than the disease. For example, property held as joint tenants with rights of survivorship, or assets passed to named beneficiaries (such as IRAs or life insurance), will not be subject to probate unless the decedent's estate is named as the beneficiary. Married couples often own virtually all their property as joint tenants, or the spouses are the named beneficiaries of each other's life insurance and retirement assets. Holding title to assets in that manner ensures that, upon the first spouse's death, there is no probate proceeding required as to those assets.

But while such rudimentary estate planning may allow the couple to avoid probate upon the first death, the ultimate result may not be so positive. When property is held jointly, the "survivor wins"— that is, the first spouse to die has absolutely no control over the assets, and the surviving spouse can do whatever he or she wants with those assets. If the surviving spouse remarries, he or she can leave those assets to the new spouse, to the exclusion of his or her own children. Even if your spouse's will or trust provides that all of his or her assets are to pass to your children upon your spouse's death, if the "new" spouse survives your spouse, then absent a prenuptial or post-nuptial agreement, in most states the new spouse can assert a *spousal right of election* to a significant share of your spouse's estate. In many states - including New York, New Jersey, and Connecticut - the spousal elective share equals one-third of virtually all assets that a deceased spouse owns at the time of death. In other states, such as Illinois, the elective share will vary between one-half of the estate (if there are no descendants) and one-third of the estate (if there are descendants). Holding joint title with children may even present a bigger problem, as demonstrated by the below example.

> **Example:** In the 2018 New York case of *In the Matter of Asch*[2], Mrs. Asch had signed a will that, like most parents, left her probate assets equally between her children, Laura and Audrey.
>
> Before her death, Mrs. Asch had added Audrey as a joint tenant with rights of survivorship of Mrs. Asch's bank accounts, which apparently contained significant sums of money. By operation of law, upon Mrs. Asch's death, Audrey became the sole owner of that bank account as the surviving joint tenant.
>
> Meanwhile, Laura, convinced that it was her mother's intent that the entire estate was to be equally divided between herself and Audrey as memorialized in their mother's will, was none too pleased that Audrey ended up with a significantly larger share of their mother's estate. Laura hired an attorney and commenced a "discovery proceeding" against Audrey as part of the probate process, seeking to prove that either (i) her mother did not have the requisite mental capacity to create a joint bank account with Audrey,

---

[2] 164 A.D.3d 787, 83 N.Y.S.3d 307 (Sur Ct, Richmond County 2018)

or (ii) that Mrs. Asch intended for the account to be a "convenience" account rather than a joint account with rights of survivorship, which would cause the account to be deemed a probate asset and thus disposed of under the terms of the will.

The Richmond County Surrogate's Court determined that the survivorship language on the account triggered the statutory presumption that the account was a joint account with rights of survivorship. The burden shifted to Laura to prove that her mother intended the account to be a true convenience account. Although Laura proved that her mother was the sole depositor of funds into the account and that the funds in the account were, with just a few exceptions, used solely by Mrs. Asch, the court determined that Laura had failed to provide documentary evidence or testimony from any person with first-hand knowledge on the circumstances surrounding the creation of the account. For those reasons, the court ruled that Laura had not satisfied her burden of proof.

On the mental capacity claim, the court determined that the medical evidence submitted by both daughters raised a question of fact as to their mother's mental capacity when the account was established. The court therefore denied each daughter's motion for summary judgment, allowing the case to continue through discovery and possible trial on that issue.

The *Asch* case highlights an all-too common scenario where an elderly parent establishes one or more joint bank accounts with a child while excluding the other children, and the parent does not understand that doing so will undermine their estate plan. In my experience, these joint accounts are established, often under the guidance of a well-meaning bank employee, simply to allow the child—who often lives nearest to the parent—to help the parent pay bills and otherwise manage their finances. But the parent could receive the same assistance from their child by simply designating the child as an agent under a durable power of attorney without the risk of "upsetting the apple cart" caused by a joint ownership arrangement. Banks, however, are often concerned that the bank would have increased liability in dealing with an agent under a power of attorney, rather than an owner under a joint account. As shown in *Asch*, however, what may be in the financial institution's best interest may well adversely affect the customer's interests, often with catastrophic and far-reaching consequences.

Merely "avoiding probate" alone is not enough. Instead, creating an estate plan that satisfies all the client's goals, including probate avoidance, should be the ultimate objective.

Personal Planning Goals: The Key to an Effective Estate Plan

Imagine building a new home *without* a set of blueprints. Sounds absurd, doesn't it? Well, it's no different than creating an estate plan without establishing planning goals; such goal setting is the "blueprint" of the estate plan.

Unfortunately, experience shows that far too often people engage in estate planning without the benefit of real goal setting. If they had, we likely would not see so many wills and trusts that lead to what are unintended consequences. For example, how many people, if asked, would want their assets to pass to their child's former spouse if a child divorced after the parent's death? Or would many people be pleased if they predeceased their spouse, only to have their spouse remarry and leave most if not all of the couple's assets to a new spouse and his or her family?

These are not questions that need only be asked by the "wealthy." For a person with $500,000 in assets or less, it may even be more critical to prevent a dissipation of those precious and hard-earned resources.

Here are some of the most common estate planning goals:

- Planning for lifetime disability and avoiding court guardianship
- Preventing a child's ex-spouse from taking the child's inheritance
- Planning for grandchildren directly
- Planning for the transfer and survival of the family business
- Disinheriting a child
- Providing for a *pet trus*t for one or more pets
- Reducing estate and gift taxes
- Appointing an appropriate health care agent and expressing your wishes for end-of-life treatment
- Protecting your children's inheritance if your spouse remarries after your death
- Planning for children from a previous marriage
- Leaving an endowment or gift for a favorite charity
- Protecting your spouse's and children's inheritance from their creditors
- Protecting *your* assets from your own creditors
- Passing on your *values* and your assets
- Protecting assets if you need long-term care

When working with an attorney to create your overall estate plan, you must address these questions, and many more. A counseling-oriented estate planning attorney will take the time and will have the training to delve into the client's goals and objectives and will help the client understand which types of estate planning documents and techniques can help accomplish those goals.

Attaining Your Goals*:* Unlocking the Estate Planner's Toolbox

There are many estate planning vehicles that an individual may use to pass assets to his or her heirs. When determining which "tool" is right for an individual, there are many factors to consider, including the size of the estate, who will receive what property and how, and the circumstances and special needs of those beneficiaries.

The first tool is the *will*. A will is a legal document governed by statute that sets forth a person's wishes as to who is to receive the probate assets included in the person's estate. Probate assets are those that are owned solely by the deceased person (the "decedent") and that have no designated beneficiaries. If a bequest is made to a minor, a typical will requires that gift be held in trust for the minor child until a certain age. In addition, a will designates guardians for minor children, and can include the person's wishes for his or her final arrangements.

A *revocable living trust* (RLT) is another commonly used estate planning tool. Trusts are contracts that create a formal agreement between one or more persons or parties to hold and administer assets under instructions in the agreement. An RLT is established during the lifetime of the trust creator (sometimes called a *grantor*, *settlor,* or t*rustmaker)*, and is administered by one or more t*rustees*, who in an RLT is typically the trustmaker, along with the spouse if the trustmaker is married. An RLT is most effective if all the trustmaker's assets (excluding retirement assets) are retitled, or "funded," in the trust name. Fully funding an RLT ensures that those assets—since they are no longer owned in the trustmaker's individual name — avoid probate, and instead are controlled by the RLT's terms.

The RLT provides an additional benefit that a will cannot: the ability to designate one or more *disability trustee*" who can step-in to administer the trust if the trustmaker becomes incapacitated or significantly mentally disabled.

Upon the death of a married trustmaker, the remaining trust assets can pass directly to a surviving spouse. However, to ensure further protection of the trust assets against "creditors and predators" of the surviving spouse, and to protect the deceased spouse's assets for the children if the surviving spouse remarries, the RLT's provisions will often specify that the assets owned in the trust will be retained in a *marital trust*, to be used for the benefit of the surviving spouse, and/or into a *family trust* for the benefit of the surviving spouse or other family members. Under present law, the marital trust / family trust structure is most relevant if you live in a state with a low state estate tax exemption amount.[3]

A marital trust will provide income to the surviving spouse and, depending upon client objectives, can provide access to the trust principal to the surviving spouse as well. Upon the surviving spouse's death, the assets in the marital trust will receive a significant tax benefit, as the assets will be "stepped-up" in cost

---

[3] The 2021 federal estate tax exemption is $12,060,000 per individual. The exemption amount is indexed for inflation and adjusted annually. Each state's estate and inheritance tax is summarized in a regularly updated chart provided by The American College of Trust and Estate Counsel that can be found at http://www.actec.org/resources/state-death-tax-chart/

basis for capital gains tax purposes. This adjustment in cost basis ensures that the marital trust assets are revalued for capital gains tax purposes as of the date of the surviving spouse's death.

> **Example:** Assume a stock originally purchased by "Tom" at $10 per share passes into a marital trust for the benefit of his wife, Mary. When Mary dies. The stock is now worth $100 per share. If the stock is sold by their children after Mary's death for $100 per share, there is <u>no</u> taxable gain to the children.

A family trust may provide that a spouse, children, and other persons will be discretionary beneficiaries of trust income and principal. Upon the surviving spouse's death, the remaining family trust assets will not be includable in the surviving spouse's estate for estate tax purposes; however, the trade-off is that the family trust assets will not receive a step-up in cost basis upon the surviving spouse's death.

Upon the death of the second spouse, the RLT will specify that the assets remaining in the marital trust and family trust are to pass to designated beneficiaries, or into further protective trusts for their benefit. This process avoids probate and allows for protection against the beneficiary's creditors, catastrophic injury, and the possibility of divorce.

Figure 1 shows a structure of a typical RLT that includes marital and family trusts for a surviving spouse, with lifetime protective trusts for the children:

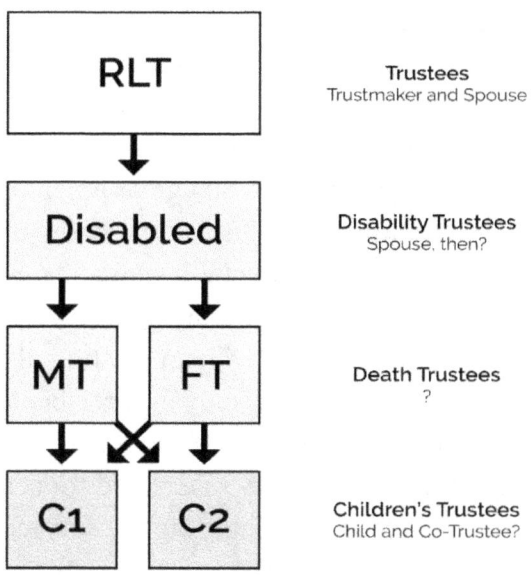

Figure 1: The Revocable Living Trust

An *irrevocable living trust* is a widely used estate planning tool to help protect assets from a "spend-down" that might otherwise be required to cover long-term care costs before a person becomes eligible for Medicaid. Assets, typically including a home and perhaps some liquid assets, are transferred to the trust; those assets are deemed owned by the trust, rather than the trustmaker who is applying for Medicaid benefits. The trust can be structured to permit the trustmaker to receive income earned from the trust assets and enjoy lifetime occupancy of a primary residence owned by the trust. All property tax and capital gains exemptions are also retained. Upon the death of the trustmaker, the assets in the *irrevocable trust* can be distributed to named beneficiaries, or often better flow into a trust for the beneficiaries. See Chapter 15 for a detailed discussion of *irrevocable trusts* used in Medicaid planning.

Both wills and living trusts can include provisions to create *supplemental needs trusts* (SNT) for the benefit of a disabled surviving spouse or any other disabled beneficiary. An SNT allows the trust beneficiary to remain eligible for government assistance, including Medicaid, without having to spend down assets to qualify for those benefits. The assets in the SNT, including any income produced by the assets, can be used for the benefit of the beneficiary as a supplement to any government benefits. This allows for preservation of assets and increased quality of life for the beneficiary seeking governmental benefits. An SNT is ideal where there is likelihood that the surviving spouse may need nursing home care, or when there is a child with an existing disability. Due to a quirk in federal law, however, only an SNT created for a surviving spouse *under a will* is deemed "exempt" for Medicaid purposes; assets held in the exact same SNT created for a spouse under a living trust are deemed "available" to the surviving spouse.

When I meet with clients to prepare an estate plan, most initially say they want to provide an outright distribution to their beneficiaries. When I discuss the benefits of leaving assets in trust for their loved ones, they are often skeptical. Their vision of a trust is usually that of a tightfisted trustee refusing to distribute assets to a truly needy beneficiary. Clients typically believe that leaving assets in trust for their beneficiaries seems to imply a form of disapproval or distrust of the beneficiaries.

Under modern estate planning, however, trusts are flexible tools, with the beneficiaries typically serving as a trustee of their own trust. A magical feature of a well-drafted trust is that under the centuries owed "spendthrift" trust rules, the trust assets are protected from the reach of a beneficiary's creditors, including a divorcing spouse. By leaving your assets in a trust for a child or other beneficiary, you can provide a level of creditor protection for them that they simply cannot provide for themselves.

In addition, a trust can be structured to ensure that assets can be left for a surviving spouse's use but be rendered unavailable to the surviving spouse's *new spouse* if the surviving spouse were to remarry without executing a prenuptial agreement. This strategy can ensure *bloodline protection* so your children and grandchildren will receive their inheritance even if the surviving spouse does not do protective planning (e.g., sign a valid prenuptial agreement with a new spouse) after the first spouse's death.

Revocable and irrevocable trusts created during a person's lifetime are referred to as *"living"* or *"inter vivos"* trusts. But one area that frequently leads to confusion is that trusts may also be created within a will, which are referred to as *"testamentary"* trusts. A common use of a testamentary trust in a will is the establishment of a trust for minor children. A typical provision might read:

> *If at the time of my death any of my children shall be under the age of 21, then the share passing to any such child shall be held in trust by my trustee, with income and principal to be distributed in the trustee's discretion to or for the benefit of such child for the child's health, education, maintenance or support. Upon such child turning 21, the trust shall terminate, and the accumulated income and remaining principal shall be distributed outright to the beneficiary.*

Likewise, a revocable or irrevocable trust may specify that upon the death of the trustmaker, the trust assets are to be distributed to new "sub-trusts" for one or more beneficiaries (e.g., a spouse or children) that are established <u>within</u> the master trust, as opposed to an outright distribution for the beneficiaries. There are many benefits to retaining a beneficiary's inheritance in trust. Assets held in trust for a beneficiary can be shielded from the beneficiary's current or future creditors, including a divorcing spouse; they can be protected from a potential spend down for Medicaid should the beneficiary someday need long-term care; and a sub-trust can specify that upon the beneficiary's death, the remaining trust assets must pass down through the family bloodline.

In my experience, employees at many banks and other financial institutions often do not understand that a trust is frequently not contained in a "stand-alone" instrument, but rather is incorporated as a sub-trust within the terms of a will or master living trust agreement. In numerous instances I have been asked by bank or financial institution employees to provide them with a copy of the "trust agreement" when in fact the trust was a testamentary trust contained within the will, or was a sub-trust incorporated within the master trust agreement. I then must explain there is no separate trust agreement, and often must work myself up the chain of command before finally reaching someone who understands that a trust need not be a stand-alone trust instrument.

Another document that is essential to a sound foundational estate plan is the *durable general power of attorney*. A power of attorney provides for one or more designated "agents" to have legal authority to handle personal and financial affairs of the "principal" who has signed the power of attorney. Powers of attorney are further discussed in Chapter 14.

Also essential to any comprehensive estate plan is the execution of various health care planning documents: *health care powers of attorney* (known in some states as *health care proxies*) authorize the named agent to make health care decisions for the person granting the authority (the "principal") if the principal cannot make his or her own health care decisions because of a physical and/or mental decline. *Living wills* (called *"advance directives"* in some jurisdictions) permit a person to specify under what circumstances the person wishes to have ongoing medical care at an "end of life" situation. And *HIPAA Authorizations* are used to designate those persons to whom your personal medical information may be shared without violating the privacy provisions of the federal HIPAA statute.[4]

What to Expect When Retaining an Elder Law Attorney[5]

Meeting with an elder law attorney is a significant step and can be fraught with uncertainty. People often come to see me in times of crisis when a parent or other loved one is in declining physical and mental health and needs help caring for their daily lifestyle needs. Before that circumstance arises, understand what the elder law planning process involves, and what your attorney will need from you to make the process the most effective it can be.

Successful elder law planning does not revolve around a particular legal document, such as a will or a trust. Wills, trusts, powers of attorney, health care proxies, and other planning documents are merely a lawyer's "tools of the trade" that achieve one or more specific planning goals. Instead, it is imperative that your attorney be able to learn as much about you, your family, the nature of your assets, and your objectives to recommend the appropriate legal strategies *and* documents designed to meet those objectives.

When scheduling your initial meeting, most elder law attorneys will ask you to complete an intake worksheet or questionnaire. The form may differ depending upon whether it is a "crisis" case where a spouse or parent needs immediate long-term care, or if it is a more

---

[4] "HIPAA" is an acronym for the Health Insurance Portability Accountability Act of 1996

[5] The term "Elder Law Attorney" is generally accepted to mean an attorney who focuses on assisting seniors and persons with special needs on a range of matters, including traditional estate planning and planning for Medicaid, veteran's benefits, and other public assistance programs.

traditional planning case where the client is looking to plan for future disability and for the disability of assets upon death. Regardless of the planning needs, these forms will typically ask for names, ages, and contact information for your children and/or other key family members. You will also be asked to provide a list of your assets, including how they are owned—individually, jointly, or payable at death via a beneficiary designation. The way assets are titled is critically important, as improper asset titling has derailed many estate plans.

Don't be put off if an elder law attorney charges a fee for the initial consultation. Elder law is a far different practice area than, say, personal injury or medical malpractice. In those practice areas, the attorney's sole objective is to bring in cases where the fee is based entirely on the ultimate settlement or trial verdict. The client never pays a fee out-of-pocket; instead, the attorney's fee, often called a contingent fee, is a percentage of the settlement or verdict amount, often one-third. Given that most attorney advertising is for personal injury law, it isn't surprising that the public's perspective about attorney fees is based largely on television ads that mention the "free consultation." Elder law attorneys are paid directly by the client for the advice provided and work performed, and do not work on a contingent fee arrangement. Elder law attorneys provide valuable advice at their initial consultations, and sometimes the advice provided at the initial meeting is all that the client needs to resolve the issue facing them.

Before the initial attorney meeting, think carefully about *what* you are hoping to accomplish.

- Is estate tax planning a major concern?

- How concerned are you about protecting assets if you someday require assistance with long-term care?

- Do you want to provide different amounts to different children, or even disinherit a child completely?

- Are you interested in making charitable gifts as part of your estate plan?

- Do you have pets you want to be assured will be taken care of?

Your attorney should discuss your planning objectives, and the different ways to achieve those goals. When we schedule an initial meeting with our clients, we provide a "Client Concerns Assessment" that allows the client to check boxes for various planning issues and concerns and serves as a starting point for that important conversation.

At the initial consultation, you should have a written list of your pertinent questions and concerns. Your attorney will be asking many questions regarding the facts of your personal situation, whether it's a crisis case or a more traditional estate planning matter. In a Medicaid crisis planning case, the attorney will need to know the health issues involved for both the client and, if married, their spouse. The attorney will also review the income and asset information that you (hopefully) have included on the questionnaire, including any gifts to children or other third parties made within the preceding five years. All such information is critical for determining Medicaid eligibility.

In a "proactive" estate planning matter, the attorney will discuss your planning goals and needs, the make-up of your family, and will often ask you to review the strengths and weaknesses of your children and other family members. You must be candid with the attorney. For example, if a child has mental illness, addiction issues, a bad marriage, or poor spending habits, that information is critical for your attorney to provide the best advice.

Think carefully about the appropriate "helpers" in the event of your disability or death. These would include executors under your will, trustees for any trusts, guardians for minor children, agents under your power of attorney, and health care agents for your health care proxy. If no suitable family members exist, you are often better off choosing a professional fiduciary, such as a bank trust department, rather than a child or other family member who is ill-suited to the task.

At the conclusion of the meeting your attorney will likely recommend a plan of action (if any) and will quote a fee for the projected work. Many if not most elder law attorneys charge flat fees for planning work rather than charging by the hour. This billing method provides the client with cost certainty and allows for open communication between the attorney and client; in my experience few things annoy clients more than getting a bill from an attorney for time spent on routine communications.

The key to a successful outcome is to embrace the attorney's planning process. Presumably you are hiring an attorney with the requisite experience, knowledge, and resources to complete the necessary planning for you. But he or she cannot do it alone, as client buy-in and cooperation is essential. A saying I learned years ago sums up my philosophy: your estate or elder law planning won't work if your attorney cares about it more than you do!

Tom Clancy's Estate: A Cautionary Tale

When novelist Tom Clancy died in 2013, he left an estate valued at approximately $86 million. While he had significant wealth at the time of his death, like many other people Clancy also left behind a blended family. Clancy had four children (hereafter the "Older Children") with his first wife, Wanda, and was survived by his second wife, Alexandra, and their young daughter Alexis.

Clancy's will left a portion of his estate to separate trusts for each of his Older Children, with another portion being left to two trusts for Alexandra, a marital trust and a family trust. Given the size of his estate and the lower estate tax exemptions in effect at the time of his death, inevitably a substantial estate tax would be owed by his estate. A significant legal issue in Clancy's estate was who would be responsible for the estate tax liability, and when would it be payable?

Had Clancy wished to defer as much of the estate tax as possible, he would have left his Older Children a total amount up to the federal estate tax exemption at the time of his death, which in 2013 would have been equal to $5,250,000, with the balance being left to Alexandra. Under federal estate tax law, assets in any amount left to a surviving spouse—either outright or in a marital trust--will pass to or for the benefit of the surviving spouse free of estate tax under a concept known as the "marital deduction". The catch is that upon the surviving spouse's death, all the assets inherited by the spouse—including any future growth on those assets—will be added to the spouse's own assets for calculating the estate tax due.

In Clancy's case, however, his original will specified that his Older Children were to receive one-third of his total estate, with the other two-thirds divided between the marital trust and the family trust for Alexandra. Under that scenario, the value of the Older Children's trusts and the family trust would have been combined to determine the total estate tax liability, which it is estimated would have resulted in a total estate tax of $15,700,000.

But shortly before Clancy's death, he executed a *codicil* (e.g., an amendment) to his will in which he modified the family trust so that the family trust would qualify for the unlimited marital deduction. The benefit of doing so was that the total estate tax bill was reduced from the $15,700,000 noted above to approximately $11,800,000. So, what could be bad about that? Well, from the Older Children's perspective, the codicil effectively shifted the entire $11,800,000 estate tax burden to their share of the inheritance; had the original will remained unamended, the resulting $15,700,000 estate tax obligation would have been divided evenly between the Older Children's share and the family trust for Alexandra, which would have effectively saved the Older Children approximately $4 million in estate tax liability.

The Maryland Court of Appeals ultimately sided with Alexandra and ruled that her husband's clear intent was to maximize the amount left to her, thereby saddling the Older Children with the entire estate tax obligation.

The Clancy case illustrates many of the counseling challenges inherent in estate planning, including some that are unique to blended families. The case demonstrates how, in larger estates, it is essential that the dispositive will or trust provides clear and direct instructions on what party or parties are to be burdened with the obligation to pay taxes from their inheritance. The Clancy case also demonstrates the potential folly in relying upon codicils to wills to change an estate plan. Such modifications often leave a trail of ambiguous and conflicting provisions between the original will and any later codicils. A far better practice is for the attorney to simply prepare an entirely new will (or restate an existing living trust if that vehicle is used), so all modifications are contained within a single instrument.

While the challenges are many, a thoughtfully conceived counseling-oriented estate plan will provide a planning solution that addresses all the client's planning objectives.

Chapter 2 - Common Estate Planning Myths

Having practiced law for over three decades, I have heard the same estate planning myths repeated time and time again. Here are some of the most common misconceptions:

MYTH: The Surviving Spouse Automatically Assumes Ownership of the Deceased Spouse's Assets.

Many people believe that by the mere existence of a marriage, the surviving spouse inherits the deceased spouse's *individually* owned assets upon the spouse's death. However, the law makes no exception for a surviving spouse. If assets are owned only in one spouse's name, upon that spouse's death his or her estate must be administered via a probate proceeding. If the decedent had a will, the assets pass as directed under the will (typically to the surviving spouse). If there is no will, then the deceased spouse's individually owned assets will pass under the state's *intestacy* rules. In New York, if a person dies with no will leaving a spouse and children, then the first $50,000 of the decedent's probate assets will pass to the spouse, with the remainder divided 50 percent to the surviving spouse, and 50 percent among the deceased spouse's children—a result that few married couples desire. In most other states the results would be much the same because default laws aim to protect both the surviving spouse and children where the decedent failed to execute their own estate plan providing for a contrary outcome.

Here's a real-world example that shows the danger in failing to engage in effective and thoughtful estate planning. I once met with a woman, who I'll call her "Barbara," about a month following her husband "Ted's" death. Also present was her daughter, "Sally." Ted and Barbara have two other children, "Alex" and "Amanda."

Barbara and Sally began the meeting by tearfully explaining that Ted had left Barbara and the family with a mess. In the early 1960s Ted started a small manufacturing business with his parents, "Roger" and "Ethel." They established a corporation, which I'll call "ABC Widget Company," to operate the business. Each of the three shareholders owned one-third of the issued corporate stock apiece.

Upon forming ABC Widget Company, they purchased a building in which to operate the business, forming a general partnership, "TER Properties," to hold title to the building. They filed a Business Certificate with the county clerk under the general partnership name as required by law. Attorneys will rarely if ever recommend that clients take title to real property under a general partnership, because in a general partnership each partner retains full personal liability for the acts and omissions of the other partners.

Throughout the years of operation ABC Widget Company paid rent to TER Properties. The company was reasonably profitable, and Ted provided well for his family.

Barbara could find no evidence that Ted, Roger, and Ethel had ever executed a shareholder agreement or partnership agreement to memorialize their respective rights and obligations upon the death, retirement, disability or other life event affecting any of them. Sally explained that her father "didn't like to deal with paperwork or deal with lawyers," so it's unlikely that he and his parents ever signed any such documents.

Roger died in the late 1990s. His will left his entire estate to Ethel, so she acquired Roger's one-third interest in both the corporation and the partnership. By the time of his death Ted was effectively running the business on his own and was keeping most of the company's profits as his salary.

Ethel died in 2006, and this is where matters became dicey. She was survived by six children and was predeceased by two children who were in-turn survived by five children of their own. Barbara believed that Ethel had a will that apparently was never submitted for probate. Therefore, as of the time of our initial meeting, Ethel's unprobated estate remained the owner of two-thirds of both the corporation's stock and the equity in the building owned by the general partnership.

I explained to Barbara and Sally that Ethel's will would still need to be probated to effectively transfer Ethel's assets, including the company stock and her interest in the building. The big question was whether Ethel's will provided that her stock in the corporation and/or interest in the partnership were to pass to Ted? If so, then if Ethel's original will were to be located and an executor was appointed for her estate, the stock and interest in the building would pass to Ted's estate. However, since Ted did not have a will, Barbara would not inherit all of Ted's interest in ABC Widget Company or TER Properties. Instead, under New York's intestacy statute, Barbara would have received the first $50,000 of Ted's estate assets, plus one-half of the remainder. The other half would pass equally to Ted and Barbara's three children.

But while that potential outcome was not optimal for Barbara, it would be far worse for her if Ethel's will—like most "simple" wills that I review—were to provide instead that Ethel's assets were to pass equally among her children and the descendants of her deceased children. Under that scenario, Ethel's two-thirds interest in ABC Widget Company and the building would be divided in *eight* shares—one each for the six surviving children, with the shares of the two deceased children to be divided among *their* surviving children. In such a case the other heirs might then seek their "fair share" of the profits earned by the business over the years since Ethel's death in 2002. Barbara could properly counter that the other heirs would be liable for a pro rata share of expenses for the business and the property. But any way you slice it, such a scenario inevitably would lead to significant expenses for legal and accounting fees to untangle the mess, plus the stress inherent in resolving complex and emotional estate issues.

While no one particularly enjoys "dealing with paperwork" or paying legal fees to handle their business and personal affairs, the consequences of failing to adequately address these issues is almost surely far more painful to those loved ones you leave behind.

MYTH: It is too late to protect your assets if you are in (or about to enter) a nursing home.

A common belief is that a person already in, or about to enter, a nursing home must "spend down" all their assets before becoming eligible for nursing home Medicaid coverage. In reality, even in such a "crisis" situation *50 percent or more* of the Medicaid applicant's assets can typically be preserved. Chapter 17 discusses "crisis" Medicaid planning techniques.

MYTH: Gifts to any individual in excess of $16,000 per year will require the payment of gift tax.

In addition to the $16,000 *annual exclusion* gifts that any individual may make to any other person (excluding a spouse, to whom unlimited gifts may be made) as of 2022, there is also a $12,060,000 per person lifetime federal gift tax exemption, which is indexed for inflation. So, it is rare that anyone making gifts will ever actually have to pay a gift tax.

Example: If a parent makes a $26,000 gift to a child, the first $16,000 of the gift would be applied against the annual exclusion amount. The remaining $10,000 portion of that gift would cause a $10,000 reduction of the parent's $12,060,000 lifetime gift exemption. If the parent had utilized no further portion of their lifetime gift exemption, then they would have "only" $12,050,000 of that exemption remaining, *plus* any additional amount added because of inflation. The $10,000 portion of the gift over the annual exclusion amount would be reported on a form 709 federal gift tax return, but no tax would be owed.

MYTH: Life insurance is "tax-free".

In most cases I review, the insured under a life insurance policy is also the owner of that policy. In such a circumstance, when the insured dies, the death benefit will pass to the named beneficiaries' *income tax* free. However, the *entire* death benefit will be includable in the insured's estate, rendering the death benefit subject to estate taxes. This rule applies even to term policies. Although with the increasing estate tax exemptions fewer estates than ever are subject to estate taxes, in those estates still taxable, the tax hit on individually owned life insurance can be substantial.

> **Example**: assume a woman who is a Massachusetts resident owns a $2 million term life insurance policy and 1 million in other assets were to die in 2022. Under current law, her estate would owe **$182,000** in Massachusetts state estate taxes.[6] If instead the $2 million life insurance policy were owned in an

---

[6] Massachusetts' state estate tax exemption is presently $1 million per person

irrevocable life insurance trust, the estate would owe **no federal or state estate taxes.**

In Chapter 12, I discuss the use of irrevocable life insurance trusts as part of an integrated estate plan.

MYTH: I don't need to create an estate plan because my estate is "simple".

A constant refrain I hear from clients is "I want to keep it simple" or, "my kids will work everything out after I die." We all seek simplicity, and hope that our children will live harmoniously after our deaths. But all too often those hopes and aspirations go down in flames without proper planning.

Example: Some years ago, I met with a widow, "Elaine," who had four adult children. Elaine owned a house in the Catskill Mountains, and another property with a mobile home in Florida. On the date of our meeting, she also had about $300,000 in liquid assets. When I asked Elaine how she wished to dispose of her property, she said that she wanted her home in the Catskills to go to one of her sons and the Florida property to go to one of her daughters, with the remaining assets to be divided equally among all the children. She explained that two of her children had been given real property on which they had built homes, and she wanted her other two children to also receive some real estate.

I asked Elaine whether the properties were of equivalent value; they were not. The Catskill Mountain property was worth about twice as much as the Florida property. I asked her how she thought her children would react if they received inheritances of differing values. She believed that her son, to whom she planned to pass the Catskill Mountain property, "would be fair" to his siblings in distributing the assets. At the risk of pouring cold water on the situation, I explained that in my experience expecting the children to work out the distributions among themselves is a recipe for disaster. Even if the oldest son were inclined to "even out" the inheritances— and in my experience, such an expectation is often unrealistic—by making any after-death distributions of assets bequeathed to him, the son would be making taxable gifts for any amounts provided to his siblings over $16,000 (or the then-existing annual gift exclusion amount) in any calendar year.

As a result of our discussion, Elaine recognized that she would not be doing her children any favors if she followed her original plan for passing her assets. Instead, she left the two children who had received no prior gifts $50,000 apiece—which she said was roughly equal to the value of the properties already given to her other children—with all remaining assets to be distributed equally among all the children. With this disposition, a child who had a particular interest in any of the properties could buy out his or her siblings at the then fair market value. If none of the children wished (or could afford) to purchase either property, then the properties could be sold after Elaine's death, with the sale proceeds divided among the children.

The attorney's role during an estate planning meeting should not be limited to simply repeating what the client says in "legal" form (i.e., producing a "boilerplate" will or a trust). Instead, the attorney should ask probing questions and test the client's assumptions by describing several "what if" scenarios. Only after reviewing all realistic possibilities can the client take reasonable comfort that the estate plan will meet their expectations of success and is more likely to preserve family harmony.

MYTH: Making a loan or gift to one of the kids won't cause conflict in the family when you're gone.

When counseling clients I am always concerned when learning that parents have made, or are proposing to make, large monetary gifts or loans to their adult children. The reasons for such gifts or loans vary. Perhaps a child finds him or herself in financial difficulty, often because of a job loss, divorce, business failure, or dependency addiction. Few parents, even those of limited means, turn away a child in need.

As the father of two children myself, I have nothing against such a parental "bailout" where a child is in genuine need. After all, family is family. But frequently I see situations where an adult child convinces his or her parents into transferring to a child a significant portion of the parents' life savings for non-essential needs, often for a questionable business venture. In a perfect world, the child should first look to a bank for financing. If a bank won't provide financing, that should be a red flag to the parent that they should think twice before providing the requested funds to a child, unless the parent is prepared to permanently part with the money.

> **Example:** My client, "Carla," had given her son, "Alex," $300,000, which Alex applied to the purchase of a restaurant. The transaction was deemed a "loan," and Alex gave to Carla a crudely drafted promissory note. However, Carla did not retain an attorney, so she did not have a mortgage placed upon the property, leaving her loan unsecured. In relatively short order, Alex's "can't miss" restaurant went bust, and Carla's chances of getting back the $300,000 loan went down the drain.

In other cases, money may be given to a child in dribs and drabs. Typically, the child in such cases has chronic financial problems, and even as an adult depends largely upon the parent for support. Sometimes the child is just unlucky in life, but all too often I see cases where a parent enables a lazy or unmotivated child to live off the parent's resources.

Where a parent is providing "help" to an only child, my main concerns are typically to (i) ensure that the parent retains enough resources to maintain their standard of living, (ii) understand the estate and gift tax implications of the transfers, and (iii) understand the implications of such asset transfers on the parent's potential Medicaid eligibility should long-term care someday be necessary. If those three issues are satisfactorily addressed, then a parent can make such transfers without significant concern.

But when there is more than one child in the picture, the situation takes a much different turn. Where parents with multiple children are financially assisting fewer than all the children, the clients should understand the potential for significant strife among their children if the parents haven't clarified in their estate plan how such lifetime payments are to be treated after the parents' deaths.

Often the most equitable approach is to provide in the parents' will or living trust that the lifetime transfer to a child is to be deemed an "advance" on that child's inheritance. That's what was done in the case mentioned above where Carla gave Alex $300,000 for his ill-fated restaurant. Carla's estate plan now provides that to the extent Alex doesn't repay the loan, his share of the inheritance is to be offset by the unpaid amount. So, if Carla's total remaining estate is $1 million at her death, Alex and his sister "Marie" would have otherwise been entitled to one-half of the assets, or $500,000 apiece. But Carla's plan provides that the $300,000 loan amount (or any remaining unpaid amount) is added to the total estate for determining each child's equitable share. If Alex's entire $300,000 loan remains unpaid at Carla's death, then Carla's total "estate" for distribution is $1,300,000, with each child to be allocated from that sum $650,000. Since Alex has already received $300,000 of that amount, he would only receive $350,000 of the $1 million from Carla's estate, with Marie to receive the other $650,000. Under this scenario, each sibling will have received substantially equal amounts of their mother's estate, including the large lifetime transfer to Alex. Such an equitable solution is far more probable to be palatable to the children and is more likely to result in harmonious sibling relations than where large lifetime gifts and/or unpaid loans are not factored into the estate planning design.

MYTH: It is not a good idea to discuss my estate planning with my kids.

Some people freely share their financial information with their adult children, and often will invite them to participate in meetings with their estate planning attorneys and financial advisers. When the inevitable occurs and the parents become incapacitated or die, the children can step in and handle the parents' financial affairs. They will have at least a reasonable idea on the nature and location of the parents' assets and will typically be designated as the parents' attorneys-in-fact under a power of attorney, and successor Trustees under the parents' revocable and irrevocable trusts. The designated children can then step into the parents' shoes and handle their personal affairs with the least possible disruption and confusion.

Other parents, however, prefer to maintain a cloak of secrecy regarding their personal and financial affairs. In one case I was contacted by a woman, "Joan" whose mother, "Hilda," had just died. Despite being in poor health, Hilda repeatedly told her children that her affairs were in order, and that her attorney (who she did not name) had all her papers. With Hilda's passing, her children were left with chaos. A thorough search of Hilda's home turned up disorganized bank account records, but no copy of a will. Joan found some keys that might have been to a safe-deposit box, but the bank where Hilda had her checking account would divulge no information to the children without a court order.

Perhaps even worse was the children's discovery that Hilda—who, remember, had her "affairs in order"—owned real estate and was on title to bank accounts with another relative, with title being held as joint tenants with rights of survivorship. Since the other relative was still living, that relative immediately took full ownership of all the jointly owned assets, including the real estate.

The children were understandably despondent about the situation left behind by their mother. As her daughter said to me at the time, "I'd like to be able to grieve for my mother—but right now I'm just angry at the mess she left behind."

The cost to untangle the mother's affairs after her death far exceeded the expense she would have incurred during her lifetime to put her affairs in order. Just as critical, an estate planning attorney would have identified the problem inherent with the mother's joint ownership of property and could have helped the woman try to re-title the assets to ensure that her children received their mother's share of the jointly owned assets.

But a person need not die to leave their family with a mess. In another case I was retained to represent a woman, "Grace" whose husband "Fred's" mental and physical health was in decline for at least two years before Grace came to see me. Unfortunately, Fred, who was then in his mid-80's, had been rather domineering throughout the marriage. As Fred's health declined, he became more difficult and verbally abusive to Grace and the children. Because Fred had been so controlling for so long, Grace was unprepared to handle both her husband and their finances. The family's only real option at that point was to file a petition to have one of the children appointed as Fred's personal and financial guardian. Guardianships can be expensive, intrusive, time consuming and emotionally wrenching for a family confronted with such a scenario. But if a parent thinks of themselves as immortal and invincible, all too often they end up in the embarrassing situation of being "sued" by their spouse and children in a guardianship action.

MYTH: Doing my own planning online is just as effective as using an attorney.

We have all seen the ads for a "do it yourself" legal website which, it is claimed, provides the forms that will allow you to handle your own legal matters without the need for an attorney. In one spot, a smiling young couple describes how they completed their own wills to protect their young daughter should something happen to them.

For those who are inclined to "go it alone," using the forms on the legal websites may be better than having no planning. With over 50 percent of Americans having no wills in place, most people can create simple wills online that will meet the basic legal requirements and will usually provide them with better results than if they have no planning in place and their state's intestacy rules were to apply.

Also, using forms created on the internet might be more cost effective for those people who would otherwise march into their attorney's office and simply <u>tell</u> the attorney exactly how the property is to pass on death, who will be the executor of the will, and so on. If the attorney simply acts as a "scrivener" and reflexively incorporates your wish list into a basic will, you probably would be paying him or her more than the cost of the legal website for essentially the same result—that is, a "word processing" document.

However, an estate planning attorney who provides true counseling instead of word processing will not simply regurgitate a client's wish list into the form of a legal document. Rather, a counseling-oriented attorney engages the client in a meaningful conversation about the client's hopes, fears, dreams, and aspirations. The attorney will ask probing questions about the client's immediate and extended family, and other important relationships, such as:

- How stable are your children's marriages?

- How well do your children handle money?

- Do your children (and their spouses) get along with each other?

- What type of philanthropy do you engage in?

- Have you ever considered what could happen to your assets if your spouse survives you and were to remarry?

- Do you have any children or grandchildren with special medical or mental health needs?

- Do you have any pets you need to arrange for if you predecease them?

- Which persons do you wish to appoint to make the determination that you are no longer capable of managing your financial affairs, and who do you want to then take over the management of your affairs in the event of your incapacity?

- Have you taken any measures (e.g., purchasing long-term care insurance) to protect your assets if you need long term care?

The list of discussion points can be almost endless, and a knowledgeable attorney will hone-in on all the key issues facing each client. Once the "family story" has been dissected over the course of several hours, the attorney will discuss how the appropriate legal "tools"— that is, the documents—can be customized to address the client's specific goals and concerns.

Accessing the attorney's knowledge and experience will initially cost more— often considerably more—than filling-in a form on a computer. But a knowledgeable and skilled attorney will provide value that far exceeds the value of any do-it-yourself planning, and the total planning costs will typically cost less once post-death settlement fees are considered. While I may be biased on this point, this bias is justified given the many horror stories I hear from people whose family relationships have been destroyed because a parent or other loved one did not create and fund an estate plan that addressed their planning objectives.

MYTH: A good alternative to online estate planning is a one-size-fits-all "trust kit".

There are innumerable benefits of engaging in counseling-based estate planning as contrasted with estate planning that comprises mere "word processing" documents. But given the vast market of people who need estate planning but who would prefer taking the path of least resistance, certain unscrupulous non-attorney "advisors" will convince their clients to purchase "one-size fits all" estate planning kits.

For instance, a local financial advisor once forwarded to me an e-mail presentation he received from a company that touted the sale by financial advisors of proprietarily named living trust packages. The email pitch was directed at the financial advisor (who is not an attorney), promising that advisors can earn, "$500 - $700 Living Trust Commissions [that] are paid fast," and that for, "every 5th Living Trust you sell, we'll send out a free 1,000-piece mailer to the zip codes of your choice." The sales pitch included the remarkable statement that the "Living Trust, for a husband and wife, contains 193 pages" (talk about one size fits all!). Finally, the company promised that "[y]ou are not limited geographically with your Living Trust business."

One slide revealed the real "benefit" to the financial advisor in selling these forms: because the advisor would presumably have access to the client's entire financial picture in order to "do" the documents, "[t]his time you'll get paid for your insurance and investment recommendations."

It is bad enough this company was soliciting non-attorneys to engage in the unauthorized practice of law. But an even bigger danger is that many well-meaning people will purchase one of these "estate plans" and believe that their estate planning needs have been addressed. These "plans" are invariably fraught with errors, and often lead to far worse results than had the client done no planning. Use of these documents might cause a loss of significant tax exemptions, and these fill-in-the-blank wills provide no customization to meet the client's actual goals and objectives. I had the opportunity to review one living trust produced from a "kit" that included language such as, "if you live in Texas, use the following clause:" and "if you live in Ohio, use the following clause …"

Besides the problems created by the "fill-in-the-blank" nature of these forms, it is almost certain that no consideration is given to proper funding of the alleged estate plan. One common selling point by peddlers of these kits is that the client's estate will magically avoid probate after their death. Unfortunately, there is probably no discussion with the client about how their assets should be titled to effectuate the client's estate planning goals. Absent a discussion about the importance of property asset titling, the client's assets will likely remain titled either in their own name (if they are single) and jointly (if they are married). Upon the client's death, or upon the death of the second spouse if the planning involves a married couple, the assets will be subject to probate, and the stated goal of "probate avoidance" is not attained.

While some may see my position on this topic as merely an attempt to protect my "turf," consider that attorneys will frequently earn far more in fees to help clean up the messes left by these disastrous "estate plans" than they would have earned in creating a sound and well-designed estate plan in the first instance.

So, if you are pitched one of these Living Trust kits by anyone—especially a non-attorney—remember the old saying: buyer beware!

MYTH: Spending the time and money to create a well-designed and implemented estate plan is not worth the hassle.

In my over three decades of practicing law, I have seen many disputes arise between and among family members after the death or disability of a loved one (or even someone not so well-loved but who may have significant assets). While the causes of such disputes may vary, a thread common to most is that the person at the center of the controversy either did no estate planning, or did rudimentary planning almost assured to fail.

Let's look at some common scenarios: A couple (Phil and Claire) with comfortable but relatively modest assets (say a home worth $250,000 plus $350,000 in the bank) signed "I love you" wills in 2011 leaving all assets to each spouse, with the three children -- Haley, Alexandra, and Luke -- listed as contingent beneficiaries. Given that the house and bank accounts are all owned jointly by Phil and Claire, when Phil died in 2019, all the assets passed automatically by "operation of law" to Claire. Claire's will (which was never changed) still provided that upon her death, her assets were to pass equally to her children. Well, what can be so bad about that? There are, unfortunately, many potential pitfalls inherent in such a "simple" arrangement.

For instance, what if at the time of Phil's death Claire was in poor health and required assistance with long-term care? In that case all of Claire's assets would be deemed available resources should Claire attempt to qualify for Medicaid to assist with her long-term care expenses. Through proper protective planning, a substantial portion of the couple's assets could have been left in a Supplemental Needs Trust created under Phil's will for Claire's benefit. An SNT created for the benefit of a spouse under a will can protect the assets left for the surviving spouse from being subject to a Medicaid spend-down.

Whether or not Claire's health ever becomes an issue, there are other risks lurking. For example, what if Claire remarried a man with a heart of gold but not much money in the bank? Given the amount of assets involved, it's unlikely Claire and her new husband, "Charlie," would have signed a prenuptial agreement. If Claire predeceased Phil, then even if her will provides that all of Claire's assets pass to her three children, Charlie may exercise his spousal right of election that would entitle him to the state's statutory share (under New York law, one-third) of Claire's estate regardless of the terms of her will. With an estate of $600,000, Charlies's elective share would net him approximately $200,000.

Another scenario: assume that Claire never remarried, and her health remained good until her death. Her will, of course, provided the assets were to pass equally among Haley, Alexandra and Luke, so they're sure to receive an equal share, right? Not necessarily; the will would only control the disposition of assets owned in Claire's name alone at the time of her death. Consider the result if, a few years after Phil's death, Claire (with Haley at her side) was doing her banking when the "helpful" teller suggested to Claire that she add Haley (who was the only child still living at home) to Claire's bank accounts so Haley could easily help Claire with paying bills and managing her accounts. Clueless as to the estate planning implications of this move, assume Clare readily agreed to add Haley as a joint owner on the bank accounts totaling $300,000.

Fast forward to Claire's death, when Alexandra and Luke are stunned to learn that Haley is now sole owner of Claire's bank accounts as surviving joint owner by operation of law. The only asset covered by the will—and subject to a three-way split—is the house. "But," they protest, "the will says everything is to be divided equally among the three of us!" The attorney handling estate administration explains that the will controls only those assets owned by Claire alone, which was solely the home. Outraged, Alexandra and Luke hire their own attorney to challenge Haley's sole ownership of the bank accounts claiming, among various possible theories, that (i) Haley was added to the accounts solely for Claire's "convenience" and the accounts did not qualify as jointly owned accounts, and (ii) Haley exercised "undue influence" in convincing Claire to add Haley to those accounts. Regardless of the outcome, the result is a shattered family and the likely expenditure of thousands of dollars of legal fees.

The moral of these stories is that "hoping" things will work out through rudimentary planning (or no planning at all) as often as not leads to unintended consequences and conflict among those whose interests you are looking to protect. Proper estate planning requires an in-depth review of your financial picture and personal planning goals with an experienced attorney who concentrates their practice in estate planning and elder law. The attorney can then provide appropriate counsel by exploring all the "what ifs" and tailoring your plan to address all the possibilities. Merely using an attorney (or even worse, a will-drafting website or software program) to serve as a "scrivener" is likely to leave your assets and loved ones exposed to any number of potential pitfalls.

MYTH: I must keep my cash in multiple banks to ensure my money is fully FDIC-insured.

When reviewing a client's financial picture, it is common to see those with large cash positions keeping cash accounts at multiple banks. When asked why they have so many accounts, invariably they say that because they wanted to maximize the FDIC insurance on their cash accounts, they spread their funds around many banks.

Having so many bank accounts, however, can cause a record-keeping headache, and can complicate matters in settling the client's estate upon their death. But utilizing simple estate planning techniques can multiply the FDIC insurance coverage many times over, allowing the client to keep all their cash accounts at a single preferred bank.

For decades the FDIC insured an individual's deposits of up to $100,000 in a single FDIC insured bank, whether held in a single account or in multiple accounts in the same bank. During the midst of the 2008 financial meltdown Congress recognized that an increase in the FDIC insurance limits was long overdue, and in October 2008 the FDIC coverage was increased to $250,000 for each individual's total deposits in a single FDIC insured bank. Although the increase in coverage was slated to be in effect only until December 31, 2009, the $250,000 amount was made "permanent" on July 21, 2010.[7]

As under the prior rules, the total available insurance applies whether the assets are held in a single account or in multiple accounts in the same bank. If an account is jointly owned, the account is FDIC insured up to $500,000. But, for those individuals who have more than $250,000 in assets (or couples with more than $500,000 in assets), revocable living trusts remain an excellent tool for increasing the FDIC coverage at a single bank.

For "informal" trust accounts—those with an "in trust for" or "pay on death" designation—the amount of FDIC insurance is determined by the number of beneficiaries listed in the various ITF or POD accounts held by the account owner at a particular bank. Under current law, there is no requirement that the beneficiaries be "Qualified Beneficiaries," which under the old rules included *only* an account owner's spouse, children, grandchildren, parents or siblings. Now naming any natural person, charity or other non-profit entity as the account beneficiary will provide the additional protection.

---

[7] The increase in FDIC coverage was included as part of the Dodd-Frank Wall Street Reform and Consumer Protection Act

Example: if Alan has a single $750,000 CD at his local bank that is designated ITF for his son James, daughter Sue, and the American Cancer Society, the entire $750,000 is <u>insured</u>, because each beneficiary's interest is insured up to $250,000. Under this same example, if Alan's wife Sally was also an owner of the account, the account could be insured for up to $1,500,000 – all at a single bank!

The rules for accounts owned by formal revocable and irrevocable living trusts are similarly flexible, with an exception for trusts with more than five beneficiaries. Assume a person's revocable living trust names five trust beneficiaries (a spouse and four children). Under the FDIC rules, the revocable trust accounts at one FDIC-insured institution will be insured up to $250,000 per beneficiary, for total coverage of the accounts in the amount of $1,250,000.

For a living trust that has more than five unique beneficiaries, the amount of protection will depend upon whether each beneficiary has an equal interest as a trust beneficiary. If each beneficiary's interest is equal, then each beneficiary will continue to be covered by $250,000 of insurance protection regardless of how many beneficiaries are named in the trust. But if the trust beneficiaries do not have an equal interest, then the total insurance will be the greater of either: (1) the sum of each beneficiary's actual interests up to $250,000 for each unique beneficiary; or (2) a minimum coverage amount of $1,250,000. For example, assume you have a trust with six beneficiaries holding $1,500,000 in a bank account titled in the trust name. Assume further the trust leaves $50,000 to one beneficiary with the other five beneficiaries to receive the remainder in equal shares. In that case the trust will provide $250,000 of FDIC coverage to the five residuary beneficiaries, but only $50,000 to the sixth beneficiary, for a total amount of insurance protection of $1,300,000.

Note that if a person maintains at the same bank various accounts titled in both a living trust and other accounts titled in their own name with ITF or POD designations, the FDIC combines the interests of all the beneficiaries the owner has designated in formal and informal trust accounts in determining the total FDIC coverage for each beneficiary.

Chapter 3 - Funding and Maintenance: The Glue to an Effective Estate Plan

Funding

When most people get around to thinking about their estate planning, they usually focus on whether they should have a will or living trust as their primary estate planning document. This "debate"—which raged in the estate planning community for years—misses a fundamental point: if people do not have their estate plans properly "funded," the type of estate planning documents they have is largely irrelevant. If assets are not owned by, or if beneficiary designations made payable to, the appropriate person, trust, or other entity, then the estate planning documents will lose most if not all of their effectiveness.

> **Example:** Assume Jerry and Sidra, a married couple with a non-taxable estate (e.g., their combined assets are below New York's' estate tax threshold, which is $6,110,000 in 2022) have as primary planning goals to ensure (i) the financial well-being of the surviving spouse and (ii) that after the second spouse's death the assets will pass to their two children and later generations of the clients' "bloodline." The couple executes a joint revocable living trust that provides that after the first spouse's death, the deceased spouse's assets share of the trust assets will pass into a protective marital trust for the benefit of the surviving spouse. After the second spouse dies, the trust provides that the couple's total assets will pass into "lifetime protective trusts" for the benefit of each child. These children's trusts are specifically designed to provide the children with access to the trust assets for their needs, while protecting the

assets if a child were to (x) divorce, (y) be sued, or (z) have a chronic or catastrophic health condition that requires long-term care.

Sounds like a winning plan, right? Well, it should be, but far too often the planning does not ultimately meet the client's objectives. Unless Jerry and Sidra take the further important step of having ownership of their assets changed to their living trust and change beneficiary designations for their retirement plans and life insurance policies, the estate planning documents are unlikely to control most or even a significant portion of the client's assets. Let's further assume Jerry and Sidra's assets consisted of the following: a house worth $250,000 owned jointly with rights of survivorship; Jerry's IRA of $250,000 naming Sidra as the beneficiary; a jointly owned brokerage account of $250,000, and Jerry's life insurance policy of $250,000 with Sidra as the beneficiary. Unless the couple and their advisors work closely to retitle these assets (called "funding"), then if Jerry dies first, the entire $1 million of assets would pass to Sidra automatically by operation of law.

This result sounds appealing on its face. There is no probate or trust administration, and Sidra has immediate access to all the assets. The downside, however, can be huge. What if Sidra were to remarry without having her new spouse sign a prenuptial agreement? What if Sidra's negligent driving caused a serious car accident, or she has other creditor problems? What if Sidra needs a nursing home or other manner of long-term care? Or, perhaps as Sidra ages, her mental capacity declines and she ends up being scammed out of tens of thousands of dollars? Since upon Jerry's death, the assets would now be Sidra's name alone, the estate assets would be fully exposed to Sidra's "creditors and predators". Under this all-too-common scenario Jerry and Sidra's children may ultimately end up with a greatly reduced inheritance.

The same result would occur if Jerry and Sidra used wills as their primary estate planning documents. Wills only control assets that are individually owned by the decedent *and* which do not have designated beneficiaries; since in our example none of the assets meet those criteria, the will's dispositive provisions would have no impact on the administration or distribution of the couple's assets. While again there would be no probate, this "convenience" comes at a serious price – *the spouse who dies first ultimately loses complete control of all the couple's assets*!

Instead, had Jerry and Sidra retitled their assets to the joint revocable living trust (or are owned outright by Jerry if the couple used wills as their primary document), then upon the first spouse's death, the deceased spouse's share of the trust assets can be protected for the benefit of the surviving spouse *and* ultimately for the children.

Funding is not a difficult task, but it requires attention to detail and persistence. The act of funding requires the client (or the attorney if the law firm does in-house funding) to notify all his or her financial institutions in writing of the proposed change. Often, follow-up communication must ensure that proper titling takes place.

Importantly, the new name on the account should not be listed as the "John Doe Living Trust." Instead, title should properly be held by the Trustee in their fiduciary capacity: "John Doe, Trustee, or his successors in trust, under the John Doe Living Trust, dated June 1, 2021, and any amendments thereto."

Special care must be given for funding certain assets, such as real property, life insurance policies, IRAs, and other retirement assets. Retirement assets should never be owned by a trust since under current law a change of ownership will be deemed a distribution of the retirement assets and cause the retirement account to be fully taxable. Instead, a trust may be named as either a primary or contingent beneficiary of the retirement account to provide maximum after-death flexibility.

If you have an existing living trust, you should periodically review whether the trust is properly funded. If you are thinking of establishing a living trust, work with an attorney and financial advisor committed to the funding process so that all your planning goals can be achieved.

Choosing the Appropriate Trustee

Over the past two decades revocable and irrevocable "living" trusts have become essential estate planning tools for many of our clients. Properly structured and funded, trusts provide a well-designed means for probate avoidance, planning for asset management upon the trustmaker's disability, and for the seamless transfer of assets upon the trustmaker's death. Irrevocable "Medicaid Asset Protection" trusts also provide a mechanism for protecting the trust assets from a Medicaid "spend-down" in the event the trustmaker someday seeks Medicaid coverage if long-term care is needed.

One critical decision a person creating a trust must consider is who will serve as the Trustee? The Trustee is the person or entity whose job is to ensure that the trust and its assets are managed properly and under the trust instructions. The Trustee has a "fiduciary duty" to act in the best interests of the trust beneficiaries and breaching that duty can cause serious consequences for the Trustee.

In a typical living trust, the trustmaker will name him or herself as Trustee, and if married will add their spouse as the Co-Trustee while they are "alive and well." Upon the trustmaker's incapacity or death, the spouse typically continues as Trustee, or if there is no spouse, one or more adult children typically step into the Trustee role. But if the successor Trustee is not adequately advised about their important legal duty to be fair to all beneficiaries, problems may arise.

The 2017 New York case of *Accounting Proceeding The Schweiger Family 2013 Irrevocable Trust*,[8] demonstrates what can happen if the Trustee does not fulfill their fiduciary duty. In *Schweiger* the Trustmaker established an irrevocable trust that allowed for income and principal distributions to be made to the Trustmaker's children only, and he named two of his daughters as Trustees. No distributions of trust principal or income could be made to Mr. Schweiger as the Trustmaker.

After Mr. Schweiger's death, his daughters serving as Trustees provided the required accounting to their siblings detailing the financial transactions from the trust during their father's lifetime. The accounting showed that during their father's lifetime the Trustees had improperly distributed trust assets to non-beneficiaries—including to their father, who was not permitted to receive trust distributions during his lifetime, and to the Trustees' own children and the husband of one of the Trustees. The Trustees' siblings were understandably upset about their sisters' "self-dealing" and violation of the trust provisions, and they filed objections to the accounting in the probate court.

The Suffolk County Surrogate agreed that the Trustees breached their fiduciary duty to their siblings. The judge not only denied the Trustees their statutory commission but imposed a "surcharge"—essentially a fine—against the Trustees for their breach. The judge rejected the Trustees' claim they were not properly advised by the attorney who drafted the trust as to their duties and obligations, and

---

[8] 2015-1642/B, NYLJ 1202799241052 (Surr. Ct. Suffolk Cty., September 7, 2017)

the judge ruled that it was the Trustees' affirmative duty to seek competent professional advice as to scope and nature of the Trustees' responsibilities.

Trustee selection has significant implications for the proper administration of any trust. As demonstrated in *Schweiger*, it is just as important that the Trustees receive proper counsel and advice as to the proper administration of the trust, especially the fundamental duty to faithfully follow the trust instructions and to treat all beneficiaries fairly and impartially.

Estate Plan Maintenance

For many people even having a simple will prepared is akin to getting a tooth pulled. Estate planning is often seen as a "transactional" event, e.g., "I completed my estate plan." Perhaps that is why it is not uncommon for many clients to *never* update their estate plan, and for those who do so, they typically wait about 20 years before revising their plan!

But to be truly effective, an estate plan must be reviewed and updated on a regular basis, even if the estate is modest. The success of every estate plan is affected by the "three L's": changes in your life, changes in the laws, and changes in your lawyer's experience.

Changes in a person's life will often have a dramatic impact on the person's estate planning. Such changes might include a new marriage for that person, a child or another family member; the birth of a child or grandchild, or the death of a family member; moving to a new state or purchasing a vacation home in another state; a dramatic change involving a family member (e.g., a child suffering a catastrophic health problem, a child joining suffering from an addiction, or a similar life-altering event); a significant increase or decrease in a person's net worth (including the receipt of a substantial inheritance); retirement; the purchase of new assets and investments; and many other circumstances.

Legal changes may also have a substantial impact on a person's estate plan. Changes in the federal and state estate tax laws over the past 20 years have had a dramatic impact on the planning for those persons with modest to significant estates. Similarly, changes in the retirement plan distribution rules may require modification of estate planning documents and/or beneficiary designations. The development of limited liability company laws and domestic asset protection trusts have provided whole new opportunities for clients in high-risk professions or businesses to better protect assets from creditors in our ever-litigious society. And the frequent changes in the state and federal Medicaid laws may dramatically affect various long-term care protection strategies commonly used today.

The final "L" pertains to changes in your attorney's experience. Any attorney worth his or her salt will strive to continually improve his or her knowledge, skills, and planning techniques. In estate planning and elder law there are any number of professional organizations and bar associations, such as the Trusts and Estates and Elder Law sections of the various state bar associations, the National Academy of Elder Law Attorneys, the National Elder Law Foundation, Wealth Counsel, and Elder Counsel, to name a few, that offer extensive continuing education opportunities for attorneys.

We tell clients with confidence that the estate plan we prepared in a prior year was state-of-the-art for its time. All the same, we advise them that since the creation of their existing estate plan, the attorneys in our firm have learned new techniques and incorporated new language in the estate planning documents that should be included in their existing planning to maintain its effectiveness and ensure the planning continues to meet the client's goals.

Changes in any of the "three L's," can erode the value of even the best-designed estate plan. To help address this dilemma, many estate planning and elder law attorneys today will offer their clients a formal annual maintenance program to ensure that clients receive updated documents and language regularly. But whether you engage in a formal maintenance program, it is imperative you meet with an estate planning attorney at minimum every few years to update your planning and address all the changes that can otherwise derail your planning.

PART II: CUSTOMIZING YOUR ESTATE PLAN

Chapter 4 - Estate Planning for Blended Families

By 2010 "blended" families became the predominant family form in the United States. Couples in second or later marriages are often conflicted with the desire to provide for the needs of the surviving spouse upon the first death, and to ensure that their own children receive their "rightful" inheritance.

Unfortunately, all too often the estate planning done by remarried couples comprises simple "I love you" wills that provide that all the couple's assets pass to the surviving spouse. Not only does such a disposition forfeit several planning advantages – including protecting assets from creditors and from a potential remarriage of the surviving spouse – but under this scenario, the first spouse to die (the "Deceased Spouse") would have no assurance that the surviving spouse (the "Surviving Spouse") will leave the assets Deceased Spouse's assets to the Deceased Spouse's children.

A better solution is typically for each spouse to establish one or more trusts to hold their respective assets. A few years ago, I completed an estate plan for a couple in a blended family, "Helen and George," who at that time were both in their 70's and had been married for 18 years. George had a son and daughter from his first marriage, while Helen had two daughters and a son from her first marriage. George was estranged from his son, Arnold, but was close with his daughter, "Diane". Helen was close with all her children, "Susan," "Kelly" and "Frank."

George and Helen were comfortable financially, but the children had varying degrees of financial stability. Susan and Frank especially were financially challenged, and George and Helen helped them out periodically. Helen owned the house that Frank lived in, and he paid the taxes and maintenance as his "rent."

George and Helen retained certain of their assets in their own names, while other assets, including their home, were owned jointly. Helen had inherited valuable real estate from her parents.

Like many couples in their age range, George and Helen were concerned about losing a significant part of their assets should either of them need long-term care. While they were both in good health when we met, they had numerous friends and relatives who had dealt with paying for long-term care, and they wanted to proactively protect at least some of their assets from having to be "spent down" before becoming eligible for long-term care Medicaid coverage should the need arise. They also wanted to be sure that their own assets passed down through their own bloodline, while ensuring the comfort and financial security of the surviving spouse. Of special concern to Helen was to ensure that Susan and Frank's inheritance could be protected from their own poor spending habits so that their inheritance could last well into their own "golden years."

Based on their goals and planning needs, the plan design included the creation of separate Medicaid Asset Protection Trusts to be funded with their real estate assets. Upon expiration of the five-year Medicaid look-back period from the date the properties were conveyed to their respective trusts, those assets are deemed "exempt" from any calculation of available resources should either or both of Susan and Frank someday apply for long-term care Medicaid coverage.

After the first spouse's death, the deceased spouse's assets would remain in trust for the benefit of the surviving spouse, with the surviving spouse receiving income from the deceased spouse's trust, but none of the principal. After the second spouse's death, the trusts were designed so that George's assets would pass into a "lifetime protective trust" for Diane's benefit, while Helen's assets would pass into equal separate lifetime protective trusts for her three children. Because George was estranged from Arnold, George elected to disinherit his son.

George had no concerns allowing Diane to be the Trustee of her own trust. For Helen the choices regarding her children's trustee selection were more difficult. After discussing the options, Helen allowed Kelly to serve as Trustee for her own trust, but Helen elected to have her cousin David serve as Trustee for Susan and Franks' trusts. Based on my recommendation, Helen created "hybrid" trusts for both Susan and Frank that specified that each of them could withdraw from their respective trusts up to five percent of the trust principal per year, with any additional distributions subject to David's sole discretion based on an evaluation of Susan or Franks' needs and other financial resources at the time of the request.

Helen's plan was also designed to provide that the house Frank lives in will pass to Frank's trust, with Susan and Kelly's trusts to be funded with other of Helen's assets to "even up" the distributions among her children.

As this real-life case demonstrates, a thoughtfully conceived, counseling-oriented estate plan, will provide couples in second marriages with a planning solution that addresses all their individual and shared planning objectives.

Chapter 5 - Planning For Loved Ones With Special Needs

Supplemental Needs Trusts

According to a 2020 report issued by the University of New Hampshire Institute on Disability,[9] as of 2019, 43.2 million people, representing 13.2 percent of the entire United States population, had some level of disability. While almost half the disabled are over 75 years of age, almost 16 million Americans between the ages of 35 and 64 are disabled, and per the National Center for Education Statistics, in 2019-20 7.3 million children between the ages of 3 and 21 receive some form of special education services.[10]

When planning for a disabled child, parents often are advised by friends—or even professional advisers—to disinherit the special needs child because, they are told, the child would lose their governmental benefits (e.g., SSI, Medicaid) if they inherited a share of their parents' estate. In reviewing existing wills and trusts of parents with special needs children, all too often I see that their estate planning documents are drafted to leave all the assets to the other children, with the expectation (or at least hope) that the siblings will take care of their special needs brother or sister.

But such a strategy leaves too much to chance. Perhaps the other siblings experience financial hardship and lose the inheritance to their creditors. They might get divorced and forfeit some of the inherited assets in a matrimonial proceeding. Or maybe they just

---

[9] https:/files.eric.ed.gov/fulltext/ED612092.pdf

[10] https:/nces.ed.gov/programs/coe/indicator/cgg

decide they'd rather keep the inherited assets for themselves instead of using it to help support their sibling.

Even if the other children will assist their special needs sibling, there are potentially negative income tax and gift tax consequences if the "well" children use the inherited funds to assist their special needs brother or sister.

While leaving assets directly to a special needs child *would* leave him or her financially ineligible for many governmental programs such as SSI and Medicaid, there is no need to disinherit a special needs child. The better option is for the parents' estate plan to include a specific share or amount of assets that is used to fund a "Supplemental Needs" Trust (SNT) established under applicable provisions of federal and state law. These "third-party" SNTs—so named because they are established and funded by a person or persons other than the disabled individual—allow for the trust assets to be used by the Trustee to supplement, but not supplant, those resources available from various governmental programs. The trust assets can greatly enhance the special needs child's quality of life by providing a source of funds that can be used for many purposes, including but not limited to vacations, electronics, and entertainment. Upon the death of the special needs child, the assets can pass to the parents' other children or descendants, or as otherwise specified in the parents' wills or trusts in which the SNT is created.

Often the parents may not have much in liquid assets to fund the SNT, and they are concerned that the special needs child will not be adequately provided for after the parents' deaths. One possible solution is for the parents to purchase a "second-to-die" life insurance policy to fund the SNT after both parents' deaths. Because these policies pay-out the death benefit only after *both* parents have died, they are often considerably less expensive than policies insuring one life only. Knowing there is a pool of money from the life insurance in place to immediately fund the trust after the second parent's death, the parents might decide to leave the bulk of their remaining assets to the other children.

Note too that an SNT for a disabled individual under the age of 65 can be established with the disabled person's *own* assets and income. Such "first-party" SNTs allow the disabled person to remain eligible for government benefits during his or her lifetime. A major difference between these first-party SNTs and the third-party SNTs discussed earlier in this chapter is that upon the death of the disabled individual for whom a first party SNT has been established, the trust assets must be first used to repay the state for public benefits paid on behalf of the disabled beneficiary during his or her lifetime. Only after the "payback" amount has been satisfied can any remaining trust assets be distributed to the remainder beneficiaries specified in the trust instrument.

In the past a frequent impediment to the creation of a first party SNT was that only a parent, grandparent, legal guardian, or a court had authority to establish a first party SNT. This rule applied even in the many cases where there was a disabled but competent beneficiary. But after years of lobbying by advocates for the disabled, on December 13, 2016, President Obama signed into law the "21st Century Cures Act"[11] that now permits competent disabled beneficiaries to create and fund their own first party SNTs without the need to obtain court approval.

SNT's are invaluable planning tools for persons with special needs. Care must be taken, however, to ensure that the SNT complies with all the statutory and regulatory requirements.

---

[11] H.R. 34 – 114th Congress (2015-2016)

ABLE Accounts

In 2014 President Obama signed into law the Achieving a Better Life Experience Act (ABLE Act). This law provides to certain people with "significant disabilities" a tool for maintaining financial resources without losing valuable government benefits.

Under the ABLE Act, a disabled person and/or their family members can contribute funds to a "529a" savings account, which is modeled after 529 education savings accounts. The contributed funds will grow tax free, although contributions are not tax deductible. Total annual contributions from all sources—the disabled person, parents, grandparents, etc.— are limited to the gift tax exemption amount ($16,000 in 2022), with the states being permitted to establish limits on the total amounts that may be contributed to the beneficiary's account. New York's total ABLE cap per beneficiary in 2022 is $520,000, while New Jersey imposes a cap of $305,000, Pennsylvania's cap is $511,758, and Connecticut's maximum is $300,000. A disabled beneficiary may have only one ABLE account, although multiple people can make contributions to that account.

A key feature of the ABLE legislation is that the disabled beneficiary may maintain up to $100,000 in an ABLE qualified account without losing eligibility for SSI or Medicaid benefits. Prior to enactment of ABLE, a disabled person would be deemed ineligible for SSI if they retained more than $2,000 of assets in their own name. Since post-tax earnings can also be contributed to an ABLE account, the flexibility of an ABLE account may encourage many disabled people to enter the workforce without the fear that their earnings will jeopardize their access to much needed public benefits. If an ABLE account were to exceed $100,000, the beneficiary would lose their SSI eligibility, but would not lose their Medicaid eligibility.

Funds held in an ABLE account can pay for "qualified disability expenses" under the statute. These permitted expenses include:

- Education,
- Food,
- Housing,
- Transportation,
- Employment support,
- Health preservation and wellness,
- Assistive technology and personal support,
- Financial management,
- Legal fees,
- Home improvements, and
- Funeral and burial expenses.

If funds in an ABLE account are used for non-authorized expenses, those funds will be subject to a 10 percent penalty on the earnings portion of the non-allowable expenses.

Any person satisfying the age criteria receiving SSI and/or SSDI is automatically eligible to open an ABLE account. If a person is disabled but is not receiving SSI and/or SSD, they may still become eligible to open an ABLE account through a certification process.

But like most legislation, the ABLE Act imposes certain limitations. Most significantly, for a disabled person to qualify for benefits available under the ABLE Act, the disability must have occurred before the person turns 26 years of age. Note, however, that a person older than 26 can still qualify for participation under the ABLE Act if the person can demonstrate that the onset of the disabilities occurred before the age of 26.

The ABLE act requires that upon the death of the disabled beneficiary, the funds remaining in that person's ABLE account must be first used to reimburse the state for public benefits paid to or for the beneficiary after the establishment of the person's ABLE account. This is like the treatment of "self-settled" Special Needs Trusts historically used to shelter the disabled person's assets so they may retain SSI and Medicaid eligibility, but which are also subject to a Medicaid "payback" requirement. Given the simplicity and tax benefits afforded by the ABLE program, qualified disabled individuals with relatively modest assets and earned income will almost certainly be better off establishing an ABLE account than a self-settled Supplemental Needs Trust.

Where an ABLE account may not prove as beneficial is when parents or other family members wish to establish savings for a disabled child or other loved one. In those instances, use of a "third-party" Supplemental Needs Trust may still prove to be the best option, since a third-party Supplemental Needs Trust can be established *without* including a Medicaid payback requirement upon the beneficiary's death, and there are no practical limits to the amount of funds that may be contributed to the third-party trust.

Under a 2015 amendment to the ABLE Act, a resident of a state was permitted to enroll in the ABLE program of any state that had implemented the ABLE legislation. As of February 2022, 45 states plus the District of Columbia had implemented the ABLE Act.

Chapter 6 - Estate Planning for Unmarried Couples

There are an increasing number of couples in long-term, committed relationships who never intend on getting married. There are many reasons for this phenomenon: maybe a partner fears losing retirement or Social Security benefits from a deceased spouse that would be forfeited upon remarriage; one or both partners may have been through a messy divorce and do not believe marriage is necessary to validate their relationship; or maybe they are not believers in the institution of marriage.

Whatever the reasons for not making it to the altar, unmarried couples face unique estate planning challenges. For those with larger estates, the "unlimited marital deduction" is not available as a planning tool. The unlimited marital deduction allows an individual to leave unlimited amounts of assets to his or her surviving spouse. The assets would be subject to estate tax only upon the second spouse's death. With proper planning, married couples can currently shield up to $24,120,000 in assets from federal estate tax and $12,220,000 from New York estate tax. In 2022, an unmarried person can leave no more than $6,110,000 to a surviving partner free of New York State estate tax. All sums over that amount are subject to New York estate tax upon the first partner's death.

What if an unmarried couple, like most Americans, never gets around to doing any estate planning? If one partner became incapacitated, the "well" partner would have no authority to handle the personal, financial, or medical affairs of the "ill" partner. The well partner might have no alternative but to file a court petition to be appointed as the ill partner's legal guardian. If there is opposition from any of the ill partner's children or other family members, the well partner's lack of legal standing might prevent him or her from gaining appointment as guardian, thereby losing all control.

If one partner dies without a will, trust, or other testamentary disposition, *the surviving partner retains no statutory rights to any of the deceased partner's property.* Under New York law, a surviving spouse, however, would retain the statutory right to the first $50,000 of the deceased spouse's assets, and one-half of the remainder of the assets (this is assuming the decedent had children, who could receive the remaining half). The laws of most states have similar intestacy rules that guarantee that a surviving spouse will receive roughly anywhere from one-third to one-half of a deceased spouse's assets.

Most states, including New York, do not presently recognize "common law" marriages, which is defined as a marriage in which the couple holds themselves out as a married couple but has not purchased a marriage license or had a solemnizing ceremony. The minority of jurisdictions that recognize at least some form of common law marriage include: Colorado, District of Columbia, Iowa, Kansas, Montana, New Hampshire, Oklahoma, Rhode Island, Texas, and Utah. Other states that do not recognize *new* common law marriages but will recognize those in existence prior to a date specified under state law include: Alabama, Florida, Georgia, Idaho, Indiana, Ohio, Pennsylvania, and South Carolina.

What are unmarried couples to do? First, they should ensure that they have well drafted estate planning documents, which typically include wills, living wills, health care proxies, powers of attorney, and possibly revocable living trusts and irrevocable "Medicaid Asset Protection" Trusts. These documents must clearly spell out the role that the surviving partner is to play as health care agent, executor, trustee, agent under the power of attorney, or other fiduciary capacity. Just as important, if the couple wishes that the surviving partner receive some or all the first partner's retirement accounts and life insurance proceeds upon the first partner's death, it is critical that the beneficiary designations for these types of assets name the partner as the primary beneficiary.

When it comes to Medicaid planning, if one partner seeks Medicaid coverage for long-term care costs, the assets and income of the "well" partner are *not* counted in determining the Medicaid eligibility of the "ill" partner. However, unmarried couples cannot freely shift assets between themselves, nor can they utilize the "spousal refusal" technique available to married couples in New York to help preserve a greater amount of the ill spouse's assets.

Planning for unmarried couples is fraught with emotional landmines, plus potential, inheritance, tax, and Medicaid traps. Unmarried couples dealing with these issues should consult with an experienced estate planning attorney to review their options.

Chapter 7 - Estate Planning For the Family Business

One of the thorniest dilemmas parents may face in implementing an estate plan is how to make sure their interests in a closely held business pass to the child involved in the business, while leaving other assets to the "uninvolved" children in a "fair" manner. Given that the family business may be the most valuable asset the client owns, providing for an equitable result can be especially challenging.

> **Example:** Assume that Myron Moneybags owns MM Manufacturing, Inc., a producer of specialized plastic tubing he founded in 1967. Myron is married to Suzanne, who has had little day-to-day involvement in the business. Their son Jeffrey has worked in the business since he finished college in 1992. Beginning in 2018 Jeffrey, who is married with three children, assumed all key management roles, with Myron having largely retired. Myron still owns all the company stock, which is valued at $2 million. While Myron is willing to give Jeffrey stock over a period of years, Myron's attorney cautions Myron that giving the stock to Jeffrey during Myron's lifetime may cause negative capital gains tax consequences for Jeffrey if he sold the company or any of the stock during <u>his</u> lifetime.
>
> Myron and Suzanne's other child, Gretchen, is a married elementary school teacher with two children. Gretchen has not been involved in the company, and Myron and Suzanne want to ensure that Jeffrey will receive the business after they are gone. But they also want Gretchen to receive an equal amount from their entire estate.

If Myron and Suzanne's total assets--including the value of the MM Manufacturing stock--equals at least $4 million, then the couple's will or trust can specify that upon both their deaths, each child will receive 50 percent of the total estate assets, with all or a portion of Jeffrey's share to consist of the MM Manufacturing stock. Gretchen would receive the first $2 million of the non-MM Manufacturing assets, with Jeffrey and Gretchen to split any remaining assets.

But the situation becomes trickier if the value of the MM Manufacturing stock exceeds 50 percent of Myron and Suzanne's total assets. One possible approach would be for Myron and Suzanne to purchase "second-to-die" life insurance that will pay a death benefit to the children upon both parents' deaths. Insurance covering two lives can often be substantially cheaper compared with a policy insuring just one life. So, if Myron and Suzanne owned non-business assets totaling only $1 million for a combined estate of $3 million, they might consider purchasing a $2 million second-to-die life insurance policy that would provide a cushion should the MM Manufacturing' stock increase in value. Under this example, upon both Myron and Suzanne's deaths their total estate value–including the $2 million life insurance death benefit--would be $5 million, with each child receiving $2.5 million from their parents' estates. Jeffrey's share would include the $2 million in MM Manufacturing stock, plus an additional $500,000 to boot.

But what if there is no insurance available to make up the "shortfall?" Myron and Suzanne will need to discuss with their estate planning attorney how their planning documents should be drafted to provide for such a scenario. For instance, they may require that Jeffrey pay Gretchen the difference in any shortfall. If the total estate assets were $3.5 million, each child's share would be $1.75 million. Since Jeffrey would be entitled to receive $2 million in company stock. Myron and Suzanne's wills or trusts might specify that Jeffrey would have to pay Gretchen $250,000, either in cash or via a promissory note payable over a period of years to equalize their children's inheritances.

Alternatively, Myron and Suzanne might decide that because Jeffrey has spent his professional life enhancing the value of the business, they would prefer that Jeffrey have no obligation to pay any difference in value to Gretchen, even if she ended up with a smaller total inheritance.

Another fundamental issue must be considered: what if Jeffrey– who in 2022 is already 51–decides that he doesn't want to be required to take the company stock as part of his inheritance, but instead would prefer to cash-out and call it a day? In that scenario it would be prudent for Myron and Suzanne to provide in their estate plan that Jeffrey has an *option* to take the MM Manufacturing stock as part of his inheritance, incorporating into their wills and trusts specific timeframes and benchmarks for Jeffrey to exercise his option. If Jeffrey decides not to exercise the option, then both he and Gretchen can receive equal shares of all their parents' assets, including the MM Manufacturing stock.

Providing for the appropriate disposition of a closely held business is a detailed process that requires the close cooperation of the business owners and their professional advisors. The earlier such planning is undertaken, the better the chance of attaining the desired results.

Chapter 8 - Estate Planning For Retirement Assets

Over the past few decades, retirement assets such as IRA's, 401(k)'s, 403(b)'s, qualified annuities, and traditional pensions, comprise an ever-growing portion of many Americans' financial portfolios. While the tax-deferred (and in the case of Roth IRA's, tax free) growth has fueled their appeal, the tax treatment associated with these vehicles can complicate the administration of an estate after the retirement account owner's death.

Retirement accounts require careful consideration in the estate planning context. Because retirement assets are subject to *both* income taxes *and* estate taxes, under the worst-case scenario, 80 percent or more of the retirement account assets can be lost to taxes upon the account owner's death.

To avoid such a devastating result, all planning options must be considered. As most people know, retirement asset distributions after death are handled through a beneficiary designation form. Despite their great importance, beneficiary designations are too often handled in a haphazard and cavalier fashion. The beneficiary designation form must be carefully completed to ensure that the beneficiaries are the proper beneficiaries in the context of the client's overall estate plan.

For instance, most married couples automatically name each spouse as the beneficiary of the other spouse's retirement account. It is true that a surviving spouse has the most flexible planning options if named as the beneficiary. However, naming the spouse outright as the beneficiary may conflict with other estate planning goals. If the retirement account is sizable, naming the other spouse as primary beneficiary might result in the unnecessary imposition of estate taxes after the surviving spouse's death, since the balance remaining in the retirement account will be added to the surviving spouse's taxable estate. And in second (or subsequent) marriage situations, a surviving spouse named as primary beneficiary of a retirement account can name whoever they like as the new beneficiary of the account, including his or her own children to the exclusion of the original account owner's children. Even in a first marriage situation, the surviving spouse may remarry and might then name their *new* spouse as the beneficiary, which would similarly disinherit the children from the first marriage if the new spouse outlives the parent from the first marriage.

So, what's a suitable alternative? The account owner might consider creating a "Stand-alone Retirement Trust" (SRT) to manage the distribution of the retirement assets after their death. The SRT can be drafted to incorporate a trust for the surviving spouse's benefit that serves as a "conduit" for passing the required minimum distributions (RMDs) annually to the surviving spouse, with the RMDs calculated each year based upon the surviving spouse's life expectancy. In this structure the surviving spouse would benefit from the retirement accounts payable to the SRT but would have no ability to direct where the balance of those assets would pass after his or her death.

In conjunction with the SRT structure, trusts for the children or other named beneficiaries contained within the SRT will typically be named as the contingent beneficiary of the retirement accounts. Under the SECURE Act, which became law on January 1, 2020 and is further described in the following section of this chapter, unless the named beneficiary falls under one of the limited exceptions, the RMDs payable to the trust for the beneficiary must be fully distributed within 10 years of the death of the original owner or the death of the spouse, whichever last occurs.

The children's trusts in an SRT will be generally drafted as "accumulation" trusts. An accumulation trust requires that funds distributed from a retirement account to the child's trust be retained in the trust until and unless the trustee elects to distribute any or all the distribution to the beneficiary as authorized by the trust instrument. The benefit of having the funds retained in the trust is that the assets are protected from the reach of the beneficiary's current or future creditors, a divorcing spouse, and will not be considered an "available resource" should the beneficiary someday seek Medicaid to pay for long-term care. One potential downside of retaining a distribution from a retirement account payable to the trust—which, except in the case of a distribution from a ROTH IRA or 401k, is treated as ordinary income for income tax purposes--is that under current law trusts have a more compressed income tax schedule than individual taxpayers. In 2022, trust income of $13,451 or more will be taxed at the highest federal rate of 37 percent, while an individual taxpayer will not reach the 37 percent tax bracket until they have $539,900 of taxable income.

But the tax issue described can be resolved so long as the trustee of the beneficiary's trust—who is often the beneficiary themself—has discretion to distribute trust income to or for the benefit of the beneficiary. If the beneficiary is not under any "threat" from creditors, is not facing a divorce, and has no immediate need for long-term care, then the retirement plan distribution may be paid from the trust in the year of the distribution and will be taxed at the beneficiary's individual tax rate. If, however, the beneficiary is facing an immediate or near-term threat from a "creditor or predator," then the trustee may elect to retain the retirement plan distribution in the trust, even at the cost of higher income taxes.

Given the additional complexity for the SRT structure, why not just leave retirement assets directly to the children or other non-spouse beneficiaries? The most important benefit of using an SRT for your children or other heirs is creditor protection. In a unanimous 2014 opinion, the U.S. Supreme Court, in *Clark v.*

Rameker[12], ruled that an inherited IRA is not an exempt asset for purposes of the federal Bankruptcy Code (11 U. S. C. §522(b)(3)(C)).

The Court in *Clark* held that a traditional or Roth IRA during the account owner's lifetime is exempt from bankruptcy because, under the statute, a retirement fund provides the account owner with a source of funds for sustenance "to provide for their basic needs during their retirement years." The Court ruled that an inherited IRA has several characteristics that differentiate it from a traditional IRA, particularly the requirement that withdrawals from an inherited IRA must begin by the year after the original account owner's death, "no matter how far [the inheriting beneficiary] is from retirement." Accordingly, the Court held that since an inherited IRA is not a "true" retirement account, it is not subject to the same legal protections as a traditional IRA funded with the account owner's own assets (or via a 401(k) rollover).

Given that retirement accounts are often the largest asset class owned by an individual, the Supreme Court's decision in *Clark v. Rameker* confirms that leaving IRAs and other retirement accounts directly to individual beneficiaries unnecessarily exposes those accounts to all the financial risks that may be facing the beneficiary—potential creditor issues, divorces and catastrophic accident or illness.

To avoid exposing IRAs to the reach of the IRA beneficiary's "creditors and predators," naming a stand-alone retirement trust to serve as the beneficiary of retirement accounts, rather than having children or other beneficiaries inherit the IRA in their own names,

---

[12] Clark v. Rameker, 134 S. Ct. 2242, 189 L. Ed. 2d 157 (2014)

can avoid the potential loss of retirement assets to creditors as articulated in *Clark v. Rameker*.

A critical component of a stand-alone retirement trust plan is preparation of a customized beneficiary designation form for all IRA and retirement accounts. If the account owner is married, the surviving spouse will often be designated as the primary beneficiary, since only a surviving spouse can perform a true "rollover" of the IRA that would become their own retirement account upon the original owner's death. The children's trust shares in the stand-alone retirement trust will then be named as contingent beneficiaries. If the account does pass to the surviving spouse, he or she would then complete a new beneficiary designation form, naming the children's stand-alone trust shares as the new primary beneficiaries of the rollover IRA. If the original IRA owner is the surviving spouse, then upon the IRA owner's death the stand-alone trust shares will be the immediate beneficiaries of the IRA.

In a blended family situation where the IRA owner's spouse is not the parent of the IRA owner's children, it may not be advisable to name the surviving spouse as the primary beneficiary. As with all estate planning, the proper planning for retirement accounts requires careful consideration of the ramifications of all planning choices available to the client. No single solution fits every client's situation and obtaining counsel from knowledgeable professional advisors is critical to the planning's ultimate success.\

The SECURE Act

On January 1, 2020, the Setting Every Community Up for Retirement Enhancement (SECURE) Act became law. The SECURE Act incorporates several significant changes to the treatment of IRAs and other retirement assets from prior law, some of which are favorable to taxpayers, and some that are not.

First, the good news. Under the SECURE Act the age at which a retirement plan owner must begin taking distributions (RMDs) from a retirement account was raised from 70 ½ to 72, allowing for additional time before taxable withdrawals must be made from the account. In 2033, the RMD age will increase to 75. Another helpful provision is the elimination of a contribution age limit for traditional IRAs for those still working.

But the most significant and negatively impactful provisions of the SECURE Act involve the virtual elimination of the "stretch" IRA. Under prior law, non-spousal beneficiaries who inherited an IRA or other retirement plan were able to take RMDs over their remaining life expectancy. For example, if in 2019 a 40-year-old child inherited her parent's $1 million IRA, the child's initial RMD would have been based on a life expectancy factor of 43,6, resulting in a required taxable distribution in the first year of just under $23,000; the remaining $977,000 in the IRA could remain in the account and grow tax deferred until the following year's distribution, when approximately 2.3 percent of the remaining IRA would have to be withdrawn from the account. Assuming the total return from the IRA were to grow at a rate more than the 2.3 percent withdrawal amount, the balance in the IRA would increase in the early years of distributions, hence the term "stretch" IRA.

Under the SECURE Act, however, a 40-year-old beneficiary who inherits a retirement account must now withdraw the entire IRA within a 10-year period calculated beginning the year after the original owner's death. Under proposed regulations at the time of this writing, in most case the beneficiary will be required to withdraw funds from the retirement account during each year during the 10-year window.

There are some important exceptions to the 10-year withdrawal rule for special beneficiaries who are designated under the law as "Eligible Designated Beneficiaries." Surviving spouses can continue to use spousal rollovers and treat a deceased spouse's IRA or other retirement plan as their own; or the spouse can elect to use their deceased spouse's hypothetical remaining life expectancy for future distributions, which is a useful option in certain circumstances, such as when the surviving spouse is older than the deceased spouse.

Another exception to the 10-year payout rule is for disabled beneficiaries, who remain eligible to use the life expectancy "stretch" payout option. For a minor child, there is also a carve-out that allows life expectancy RMD's to be paid to the minor child until they reach the "age of majority" (which in New York and many other states is 18), at which time the 10-year payout rule will apply for the balance of the retirement account.

For cases involving Eligible Designated Beneficiaries, upon the death of any of *those* specified beneficiaries, the 10-year rule then kicks-in for distributions to the next-level beneficiaries.

Where there are no Eligible Designated Beneficiaries and a lifetime stretch-out is still desired, one option—which is especially appealing for those who are charitably inclined--is to name a Charitable Remainder Trust (CRT) as the beneficiary of the retirement account. In this structure, the retirement plan is paid to the CRT upon the plan owner's death. Since the CRT is a non-taxable trust, there is no 10-year payout requirement. The IRA owner's beneficiaries (typically their children) can then receive annual payments (which will constitute taxable income for the most part) from the CRT over their lifetime, thereby "mimicking" the stretch IRA. Upon the income beneficiary's death(s), the remaining assets in the CRT must be paid to one or more charitable beneficiaries.

While the accelerated withdrawal period required in most cases under the SECURE Act may be good for the U.S. Treasury, it will increase the tax burden on millions of Americans. Trusts remain valuable planning tools for inherited IRAs for many types of beneficiaries, especially if protecting inherited IRAs from the reach of a beneficiary's creditors or preserving public benefits for a disabled beneficiary is an important planning goal. It is important for anyone with retirement accounts of more than nominal value to meet with an experienced estate planning attorney to review their beneficiary designations and to decide if a stand-alone retirement trust should be incorporated as part of their estate plan.

Chapter 9 - More Specialty Planning Topics

Planning For Your Pets

For many people a pet is their closest and dearest family member. Without careful planning, however, your pets may not receive your desired care and treatment upon your disability or death. According to the Society for the Prevention of Cruelty to Animals, if a pet is deemed abandoned for at least 10 days, a written notice is provided to the owner at their last known address, with the animal to be delivered to the nearest humane society or animal shelter.

To avoid that result, pets can be included as an integral part of an estate plan. Your power of attorney can provide an explicit power authorizing your designated agent to provide for the care of your pets. In your living trust, health care proxy and living will, you may state your intention to have your pets remain with you if it is feasible.

Contingency plans should also be made if an emergency occurs. First, find at least two responsible friends who will be temporary caregivers, and make sure their phone numbers are available to friends and neighbors. Second, carry an alert card in your wallet or purse listing the emergency caregivers. And third, post decals on the doors and windows of your home alerting emergency personnel there are pets in the home.

One dilemma is how to provide financially for your pets if they should survive you? Under New York law (and the law of many other states), you may create an express pet trust to provide a source of money to pay for the care and feeding of your pets after your death. New York's Estates, Powers, and Trusts Law §7-8.1 authorizes a pet owner to set aside funds in a trust to be used by a designated individual (or an individual appointed by a court if no named individual is available) for the benefit of pets. The statute provides that the trust must terminate when no living animal is covered by the trust, or at the end of 21 years, whichever occurs first. Upon the trust termination, the remaining income and principal may pass to beneficiaries designated in the trust, or if none, to the trustmaker's estate. Note that if a court determines that a trust is funded with an amount that substantially exceeds the sum required for the intended use, the court may reduce the amount of the property transferred to the trust.

A terrific resource for pet owners is the book *All My Children Wear Fur Coats,* written by Peggy Hoyt, a Florida estate planning attorney. Peggy's book provides an easy-to-read road map for pet owners on how to integrate your pets as part of your estate planning. You can learn more at www.legacyforyourpet.com.

Planning For a Vacation Home

For many families their favorite memories include gatherings at the family vacation home, whether it's on a lake, in the mountains, at the shore, or at points in between.

While mom and dad are around, they will be the final arbiters regarding use of the vacation home by the children and other family members. The parents serve as the essential "glue" that keeps the peace among potentially fractious children (not to mention the children's spouses).

But what happens after the parents are gone? If the parents hope that the vacation home will remain "in the family" for future generations, then the typical "simple" will that leaves that property equally to the children after both parents' deaths is likely not the answer. Often the children will find themselves in different economic and geographic situations. Suppose one child lives 50 miles from the vacation home, while another child lives five hundred miles away. It is probable that the more distantly located child will have less opportunity to use the vacation home. Perhaps that child will tell his siblings, "well, I'm not using it anyway, and I can't afford the property taxes--let's just sell the place." If the other children want to keep the home, but the reluctant child doesn't contribute for taxes or other expenses, friction between the siblings is almost guaranteed.

The situation gets even murkier if the property passes to the succeeding generations. What if child #1 has three children and child #2 has only one child? As title to the property passes to the grandchildren, the three children of child #1 will divide their parent's 50 percent share, while child #2's daughter will inherit her parent's entire 50 percent share. In that scenario disputes will likely arise over issues such as usage of the property and the financial contributions expected from the various owners.

While such potential trouble spots abound, there are viable ways for the parents to plan to keep the vacation home in the family for generations to come. The parents should consider placing the vacation home into either a "vacation home trust" or a limited liability company (LLC). Both planning tools have similar features. After the parents' deaths, title to the vacation home would not pass to the children; rather, the home would remain titled to the entity, with the trust agreement or LLC operating agreement specifying the family members' rights and responsibilities, through all the generations.

Here's an example of how a vacation home transferred to an LLC can be managed. Assume Paul and Claire Dough own a lakefront cabin in the Adirondacks. Paul and Claire have three children, Robert, Susan, and Amy. Paul and Claire form "Dough Family Property LLC," and transfer title to the vacation home to the LLC. In the LLC operating agreement Paul and Claire specify that each of their children--regardless of how many children any child may have--would be allocated a single "voting unit" on all major decisions affecting the vacation home. Each child's single voting unit could be passed on to their respective children, so no child would be benefited by, or disadvantaged from, having more or fewer children than their siblings. The operating agreement also provides for a "lottery" of preferred dates for uses of the home, with each child (or their offspring) getting first choice annually on a rotating basis. The operating agreement also provides for "penalties" if one of the family "branches" fails to pay property taxes or other expenses. In the Dough's case, these penalties as specified in the operating agreement include restrictions on use of the home, as well as the dilution of the defaulting heir's membership interest upon an uncured default of a financial obligation owed to the LLC.

The provisions that can be included in a vacation home trust or LLC agreement are limited only by the imagination of the parents and their estate planning advisor. But failing to address this critical planning issue is almost certain to lead to the end of the family retreat—and may even result in a permanent rupture of the children's relationships.

Planning For a Non-Citizen Spouse

Many married couples are familiar with the idea that upon their death they can leave unlimited amounts of assets to a surviving spouse without those assets being subject to federal or state estate taxes. One estate planning technique is to pass assets of the first spouse to die into a family trust in a sum up to the current federal estate tax exemption amount ($12,060,000 in 2022), with the balance being passed to the surviving spouse, either outright or in a marital trust. In this scenario, upon the surviving spouse's death only those assets passing directly to the surviving spouse, or into a marital trust for the surviving spouse's benefit, are subject to estate taxes. But with today's large estate tax exemptions, it is often recommended that in all but truly large estates for the deceased spouse's assets to pass into a marital trust for the surviving spouse, which ensures that the assets in the martial trust receive a step-up in cost basis for capital gains tax purposes upon the surviving spouse's death.

These rules, however, do not apply where the surviving spouse is not a United States citizen. In 1988, Congress passed legislation to remedy what it perceived was an abuse of the tax system. The perception was that many non-citizen spouses were, after the death of the citizen spouse, returning to their homelands and avoiding the United States estate tax system. The 1988 legislation eliminated the Unlimited Marital Deduction for property over $100,000 where the property passed from a U.S. citizen to a non-citizen spouse. This rule can have a drastic impact on the surviving spouse, often forcing a liquidation of assets to pay the estate taxes due within nine months after the death of the citizen spouse.

One ready solution to this problem is to implement an estate planning device called a *Qualified Domestic Trust* (QDOT)[13]. As the technical requirements are satisfied, use of a QDOT permits assets to pass into a trust for the surviving non-citizen spouse in a manner that will allow that spouse to utilize the Unlimited Marital Deduction. In its basic form, a QDOT allows for distributions of income to the surviving spouse (and distributions of principal because of "hardship") without being subject to estate tax. Distributions of principal from the QDOT to the surviving spouse (other than hardship distributions) are subject to estate taxes calculated at the marginal estate tax rate of the deceased spouse's estate.

---

[13] QDOTs are authorized under 26 U.S. Code §2056A

A QDOT may be established as part of the estate plan of the deceased spouse, or even by the surviving spouse if the QDOT is formed by the time an estate tax return must be filed (ordinarily nine months after the first spouse's death, but that time frame is automatically extended to fifteen months upon filing for an extension).

Some of the key requirements of a QDOT are (i) at least one Trustee must be an individual U.S. Citizen or U.S. corporation; (ii) the U.S. Trustee must be able to withhold taxes due on distributions of trust principal; and (ii) the executor or trustee of the deceased spouse's estate must make a QDOT election to qualify the QDOT for the Unlimited Marital Deduction.

One complication with a QDOT is the impact of the spousal portability rules discussed in Chapter 10. While the rules are complicated, the essential issue is that a non-U.S. spouse who is the beneficiary of a QDOT may have included in the non-U.S. spouse's taxable estate the "unused" portion of the deceased spouse's federal estate tax exemption but may not utilize the deceased spouse's unused estate tax exemption to offset any of the non-U.S. spouse's gift tax liability.

Marital Agreements

While marital agreements in the form of prenuptial or post-nuptial agreements are most often used in second or subsequent marriages, they can also be used for other purposes, including where a married couple hopes to ensure that the children receive their "rightful" inheritance after both spouses have died. With most boilerplate "I love you" wills that couples typically execute, the couple's combined assets pass to the surviving spouse, giving the surviving spouse full control over the ultimate disposition of the assets. Since it is unknown which spouse will survive the other, the couple may be concerned with how to ensure that the surviving spouse does not leave the assets to someone else—such as a new spouse or paramour--rather than to the couple's children.

One technique available to presumptively ensure that the surviving spouse will leave the marital assets to the children is a signed marital agreement specifying that the surviving spouse's will must leave all assets to the couple's children upon the death of the surviving spouse.

Such a marital agreement was the subject of a 2017 New York case, *Tretter v. Tretter*[14]. In May 1997 Agnes and Vitus Tretter signed a marital agreement requiring that each spouse's will leave all assets to the surviving spouse, and then to the couple's children equally. Vitus died in July 1997, and Agnes inherited all of Vitus's assets, which included parcels of real estate worth several million dollars.

In 2014 one of Agnes's sons, Edward Tretter, sued his mother alleging that Agnes violated her agreement with Vitus by gifting some of the real estate to her other two children, and by changing the beneficiaries under her will. But the appellate court affirmed the trial court's dismissal of Edward's complaint, with the appellate court holding that (i) nothing in Vitus's and Agnes's agreement prohibited the surviving spouse from making *lifetime* gifts that differed from the disposition under the will; and (ii) Edward's assertion that his mother's modification of her will violated the marital agreement was premature, as any such action could be brought only *after* his mother's death when the will was submitted for probate.

While the court's ruling was correct as a matter of law, the fact remains that Agnes's actions violated the intent of the marital

---

[14] 150 A.D.3d 1039, 55 N.Y.S 3d 301 (2d Dep't 2017)

agreements. So, how could Vitus—who because he died so soon after the marital agreement was signed, likely was then terminally ill—have better protected Edward's interests? For starters, Vitus and Agnes should have specified in the marital agreement that no lifetime gifts of the assets could be made <u>unless</u> the gifts were made equally to each child.

Another option would have been for Vitus and Agnes to have created one or more limited liability companies (LLCs) to take title to their valuable real estate, with Vitus and Agnes being the initial members of each LLC. Besides providing the Tretters with significant asset protection in the event of third-party claims brought against any of the properties, the operating agreements for the LLCs could have been drafted to restrict any member from conveying their membership interest during their lifetime, unless transfers were made equally to all the children.

Vitus and Agnes also could have established living trusts to which their property would have been transferred during their lifetime. The trusts could have been drafted to provide that upon the first spouse's death, the property would continue to be held in a "QTIP"[15] trust to benefit the surviving spouse—with the survivor having no authority to distribute trust assets during their lifetime-- and upon the surviving spouse's death, the property would then be distributed equally among the children.

The Tretters clearly had better planning options available to ensure the desired planning result. Instead, their poorly drafted marital agreement resulted in the frustration of Vitus's stated planning goals, not to mention the unseemly spectacle of a child suing a parent.

---

[15] QTIP trusts further discussed in Chapter 19

PART III: ESTATE & GIFT TAXES

Chapter 10 - The Skinny on Estate Taxes

Federal Provisions

While an estate plan that satisfies the client's personal planning goals differentiates the effective estate plans from the mediocre ones, there's no escaping that clients must always be assured that the plan will help minimize estate taxes. The good news is that in December 2010, President Obama signed into law the Tax Relief, Unemployment Reauthorization, and Job Creation Act of 2010[16]. This law dramatically changed the federal estate & gift tax rules but was slated to be in effect for only two years. However, in 2013 this estate and gift tax structure was finally made "permanent." Here are the key features of the federal estate and gift tax rules:

- The individual exemption amount for estate, gift and generation-skipping tax was set at $5 million per person, with that figure indexed for inflation. The exemption amount in 2022 is $12,060,000 per person.

- The top estate, gift and generation skipping tax rate is 40 percent.

- The law provides for "portability" of the individual estate tax exemption from one spouse to another; that is, a decedent's executor can transfer any unused exemption amount to the surviving spouse without the requirement that the deceased spouse's exemption amount pass into a credit shelter trust.

- The estate and gift tax exemption was "reunified," meaning that use of any portion of a person's gift tax exemption

---

[16] Pub L. 111-312

during lifetime results in a corresponding reduction in his or her remaining estate tax exemption at death.

Portability

The spousal portability rule was the most dramatic change produced by the statute. Prior to 2011, a married couple would "forfeit" the estate tax exemption of the first spouse to die if, like with most couples, the surviving spouse directly inherited all the deceased spouse's assets. The only way to preserve the deceased spouse's federal estate tax exemption was to fund all or a portion of the deceased spouse's assets into a credit shelter trust. A frequent complaint about this arrangement was that in requiring a couple's estate plan to incorporate credit shelter trusts to take advantage of each spouse's estate tax exemption, the law made estate planning "too complicated." In response to these concerns, effective January 1, 2011, Congress enacted legislation[17] that allowed a surviving spouse to "add" to the surviving spouse's estate tax exemption any portion of the deceased spouse's unused estate tax exemption. Portability provides a mechanism that allows a couple to take full advantage of each spouse's federal estate tax exemption without the use of a credit shelter trust, regardless of how the deceased spouse's assets pass to the surviving spouse. Under the "portability" rules, the surviving spouse can inherit the deceased spouse's asset outright and still utilize the deceased spouse's estate tax exemption by entering the appropriate information on a federal form 706 estate tax return.

Example: a married couple with a $10,900,000 estate did no estate planning besides taking title to all their

---

[17] Tax Relief, Unemployment Reauthorization, and Job Creation Act of 2010 (the "2010 Act). With portability due to expire when the 2010 Act was to "sunset" on December 31, 2012, Congress made portability "permanent" in the American Tax Relief Act of 2012, which became law on January 1, 2013.

assets as joint tenants with rights of survivorship. Assume that the husband died in January 2016 and then the wife died a month later. If the portability rules did not exist, the husband's $5,450,000 federal estate tax exemption would have been "lost," since upon the wife's subsequent death, her executor could have only applied the wife's $5,450,000 estate tax exemption against the total $10,900,000 combined estate now part of the wife's estate. Without portability, the estate for the surviving spouse, who essentially inherited the first deceased spouse's $5,450,000 estate (one-half of the $10,900,000 total) would have been saddled with a whopping federal estate tax obligation of approximately $2,144,000.

With that advent of portability, however, the executor of the surviving spouse's estate would file a federal 706 estate tax return in which a portability election would be made to take full use of the first deceased spouse's federal estate tax exemption. By simple use of that election, the entire $10,900,000 estate can pass to the wife's heirs without the imposition of any federal estate tax.

Notwithstanding the portability option, there are many cases where use of a credit shelter trust will provide significant non-tax related benefits to the surviving spouse and children, including: remarriage protection; creditor protection; and protection for the children's inheritance in "blended" family situations.

While portability is a nice option when other planning has not been utilized, it should be seen merely as a "last resort" planning device and should *not* be a substitute for a well-designed estate plan. What if, using the above example, the couple was in a second marriage and each spouse had children from their prior marriage? Because the wife was the surviving spouse, the entire $10,900,000 estate would pass solely to her heirs, with nothing to the husband's heirs. It would be small consolation to the husband's heirs that use of portability saved the wife's heirs from having to pay any federal estate taxes! Also, portability may not apply to a state's estate tax exemption, which is the case under New York law.

Finally, having assets pass directly to a surviving spouse and relying on portability to "solve" the federal estate tax issue leaves inherited assets exposed to (i) claims of the surviving spouse's creditors, (ii) a possible divorce if the surviving spouse remarries, and (iii) potentially huge future long-term health care expenses if the surviving spouse someday needs long-term health care. In each scenario, the well-planned use of trusts for the benefit of a surviving spouse and other family members can both maximize each spouse's estate tax exemptions under both federal and state laws and provide essential protections against "creditors and predators" who may someday prey on the surviving spouse.

State Estate & Inheritance Taxes

As of 2021, these jurisdictions had their own estate and/or inheritance taxes: Connecticut, District of Columbia, Hawaii, Illinois, Iowa, Kentucky, Maine, Maryland, Massachusetts, Minnesota, Nebraska, New Jersey, New York, Oregon, Pennsylvania, Rhode Island, Vermont, and Washington.

New York's Estate Tax

On April 1, 2014, Governor Andrew Cuomo signed into law the first significant changes to New York's estate tax in almost fifteen years. The law expanded New York's estate tax exemption and significantly reduced the number of New York estates subject to a state estate tax. With an eye towards being more competitive with other states, the increase in the New York State estate tax exemption was phased in over five years:

For deaths between:

- April 1, 2014 to March 31, 2015—$2,062,500 exemption
- April 1, 2015 to March 31, 2016—3,125,000 exemption
- April 1, 2016 to March 31, 2017—$4,187,500 exemption
- April 1, 2017 to December 31, 2018—$5,250,000 exemption

Beginning on January 1, 2019, the New York estate tax exemption was indexed for inflation. In 2022, the New York estate tax exemption is $6,110,000 per decedent.

While the 2014 law provided immediate and rapidly accelerating relief for most New York estates, estates of decedents with assets over the then-applicable state exemption amount may be in for a rude surprise because of what practitioners are referring to as the estate tax "cliff". Specifically, if the decedent's taxable estate is between 100 and 105 percent of the New York exemption then in effect, the result will be the *loss* of the *entire* applicable exemption, and the estate will owe a New York estate tax on the full value of the estate from the first dollar.

> **Example:** in 2022 New York's estate tax exemption is $6,110,000. If a New York resident died that year with a taxable estate of $6,160,000—which was just $50,000 more than the $6,110,000 exemption amount —then the New York estate tax due is $126,480, which is an effective estate tax rate of $253 percent!

A further twist is that gifts made within three years of death will be *added back* to the decedent's taxable estate unless the decedent was not a New York resident when the gift was made. This rule applies even to gifts of real estate and tangible personal property located *outside* of New York State, even though such property would not have been subject to New York estate tax had the decedent owned the gifted property at the time of her death.

A solution to the New York "cliff" is to include a provision in your will or living trust known as the "Santa Clause." The Santa Clause allows the Executor or Trustee to pay any amounts that would be subject to the cliff to one or more charities. In the above example, if the fiduciary donates to charity the $50,000 amount which exceeded the New York exemption, there would be no New York estate tax due, with the family receiving $76,480 more than if no charitable donation were made.

Chapter 11 - Gift Taxes & the Effective Use of Gifts

People typically are aware that there is an annual gift tax exclusion afforded under Federal law. In 2022, the gift tax exemption is $16,000 per year, per donee. The donee is usually a child or grandchild, but the donee need not be a relative. Married couples can use "gift splitting" to double the gift per donee, up to $32,000 per year. Besides the annual gift exclusion amount, in 2022 each person possesses a $12,060,000 lifetime gift tax exemption. Gifts over the annual exclusion amounts will simply reduce the lifetime gift exemption and will require filing a form 709 Federal gift tax return.

> **Example:** if in 2022 a single person makes a gift to a child of $26,000 in a calendar year (assuming there have been no prior taxable gifts), $16,000 of the gift would be attributed to the annual exclusion, while $10,000 would be applied as a reduction of the lifetime $12,060,000 exemption, leaving a remaining lifetime exemption of $12,050,000. Only after the entire $12,060,000 exemption was exhausted would there be any requirement that the donor pay any Federal gift tax.

New York abolished the state gift tax in 2000. As of 2022 Connecticut was the only state that retained its own gift tax, but the Connecticut gift tax exemption amount for 2022 is a robust $9,100,000.

Gifting is attractive for many reasons. People often look to help a child or grandchild who may have a specific need, such as purchasing a home. Gifting is also helpful in reducing estate tax exposure for taxable estates; every dollar transferred to a child or grandchild also transfers all appreciation for that asset from the donor to the donee.

Besides the annual and lifetime gift exclusion amounts, donors can provide for qualified educational expenses or medical expenses for children, grandchildren, or other beneficiaries. With tuition bills going through the roof, these gifts can go a long way towards not only assisting a family member, but also in reducing a potential estate tax bill.

While outright gifting has some appeal, there are some real drawbacks. First, an outright gift means the donor must actually part with the money–something that sounds reasonable in theory, but it is not as appealing to many people when it's time to actually make the gift. Gifting may also affect the donor's potential Medicaid eligibility, even if at the time of the gift the donor had no intention of ever needing Medicaid to pay for long-term care expenses. For nursing home Medicaid purposes, applicants will be penalized for most asset transfers made within five years of applying for Medicaid. Chapter 17 includes a more detailed discussion of gifts in the context of Medicaid planning.

Another drawback of outright gifts is the potential capital gains tax implications. Under present law, if assets are held until death, they receive a "step up" in tax basis to the date of death value, and the heirs may pay little if any capital gains tax when the asset is sold. Conversely, gifted assets take a "carryover" basis, where the donee would recognize the same gain on sale as would the donor.

> **Example:** assume a parent owns stock purchased in 1980 for $10 per share that is worth $100 per share upon the parent's death. If a child who inherits the stock then sells the stock for $100 per share, the child recognizes no gain on the sale and would pay no capital gains taxes. If, however, the stock had

been gifted to the child during the parent's lifetime and the child later sells the stock for the same $100 per share, the child, if a New York resident, will pay combined federal and state capital gains taxes on the $90 gain (i.e., the difference between the sale price of $100 and the cost basis of $10) of up to 31.4 percent (or approximately $28.26 per share).

529 Education Savings Plans

So, if an outright gift does not make sense in many cases, what are the alternatives? One option is a 529 college savings plan. A 529 plan is an educational saving program authorized by Congress in 1996 to help families save for future college costs. Every state has one or more 529 plans in place. The plans are typically established for the benefit of a child or grandchild, but can also be established for nieces, nephews, or other "permitted beneficiations" as specified in the Internal Revenue code. Once the plan is in place, contributions are made to the account. The investments in the plan grow free of federal income tax, and New York residents who use the New York 529 plan can receive a tax deduction of up to $5,000 per year ($10,000 for those that are married and file jointly). Previously, only the owner of the plan could contribute to their 529 account, but in 2008 New York enacted legislation that allows a non-owner to contribute to a 529 plan; however, the non-owner cannot claim a New York State income tax deduction for his or her contribution.

When funding the plans, in 2022 the donor could utilize their annual gift tax exclusion and contribute $16,000 (or $32,000 for a married couple) per beneficiary without depleting their unified credit or incurring a gift tax. 529 plans also offer a special five-year election, where an individual can contribute as much as $75,000 to a plan (or $150,000 for a married couple), provided that no other gifts utilizing the annual exclusion are made to the same beneficiaries during the five-year election period. However, there is a limit on how much can be gifted to a 529 plan. In New York, as of 2022 the aggregate value of gifts made to the plan cannot exceed $520,000.

Under the tax code, contributions to the plans are considered completed gifts. Therefore, once a donor contributes to the plan, those monies are no longer "owned" by the donor but are outside their estate for estate tax purposes. While the plan owner must give up all control over the gifted funds to have them excludable from his or her estate, the plan owner retains the authority to change the beneficiary of the plan to a "qualified family member," who may be another child, grandchild, or other qualified family member.

Besides the tuition assistance provided by the 529 plan funds, there are additional benefits to the beneficiary. If the plan owner is someone other than the beneficiary's parent, the assets in the plan will not negatively affect the beneficiary's ability to obtain financial aid and need not be disclosed on financial aid applications. However, if the plan is owned by a parent, the assets in the plan must be reported on the federal financial aid application (FAFSA).

When considering a 529 plan, many people are concerned about what happens to the assets in the plan if the beneficiary does not go to college. The plan owner has two options: they can change the beneficiary to another qualified family member who is or will be attending college or other qualified educational institution, or they can take the money out of the 529. If the money is taken out of the 529 plan, any earnings on the growth will be taxable to the plan owner at his or her ordinary income tax rate, plus a 10 percent penalty.

As part of a comprehensive estate plan, a structured 529 gifting program may be an excellent way to reduce the value of an individual's taxable estate, while providing much needed educational support for grandchildren and other family members.

Gifting Trusts

Although 529 plans are appealing, the investment performance of some plans has been less than stellar. Furthermore, if withdrawn funds are not used for educational purposes, they are subject to a 10 percent federal tax penalty, and may be subject to state tax penalties. As an alternative to the 529 plan, parents and grandparents may consider using an irrevocable "gifting" trust for minors. The trust is created by the parents or grandparents, usually naming a trusted family member (e.g., the minor beneficiary's parent) or professional advisor as the Trustee. While a single trust can be created for multiple grandchildren, it is usually more efficient to create separate trusts for each grandchild to whom gifts are to be made.

Once the trust is established, gifts can be made to the trust, often in an amount that does not exceed the annual gift tax exemption amount ($16,000 per donee in 2022). Ordinarily, gifts made into a trust are not considered gifts of a "present interest," and do not qualify for the annual gift tax exemption. However, so long as the trust provides that (i) the Trustee may make distributions of income and principal for the minor's benefit and (ii) all trust assets must be distributed to or for the benefit of the minor beneficiary by the beneficiary's 21st birthday, the trust gifts will qualify for annual gift tax exemption.

But many parents and grandparents fear the potential of "affluenza" if children or grandchildren were to receive large lump-sum distribution at age 21 and would prefer that the trust remain in place beyond the beneficiary's 21st birthday. To prevent a large potential windfall for a beneficiary who turns 21, the trust can be drafted to provide that upon attaining the age of 21, the trust beneficiary possesses the right to withdraw all or part of the trust assets within a certain limited period (often 30 days). If the designated time period elapses and the withdrawal right has not been exercised, the assets may remain in the trust, with specific instructions provided to the Trustee regarding how the trust assets may be utilized; if the beneficiary hopes to receive future gifts from a parent or grandparent, they would be wise not to exercise the withdrawal right.

The Trustee may be afforded complete discretion to use the trust assets for any need of the beneficiary. Distribution options may be more narrowly tailored to specific "needs" (typically health, education, and maintenance). The trust can also permit the beneficiary to become a Co-Trustee upon reaching a designated age, thereby allowing a "training period" for the beneficiary to learn how to manage his or her assets. Finally, assets in a properly structured "gifting" trust will be protected from the beneficiary's future creditors, including a divorcing spouse.

Gifting trusts for minors are underutilized planning tools. They provide more flexibility than 529 plans in making distributions to or for the beneficiary, but minor's trusts also permit a greater range of investment choices. And, if drafted with the "hybrid" language allowing the trust to continue beyond age 21, these vehicles can be effective lifetime gifting vehicles.

PART IV: ASSET PROTECTION - LIFE INSURANCE & MORE

Chapter 12 - Integrating Life Insurance With Your Estate Plan

Life Insurance Basics

Life insurance is typically purchased for two primary purposes: providing vital income replacement upon the death of a "breadwinner," and covering some or all the cost of estate taxes for larger estates.

Unfortunately, many people are not aware that if life insurance is not properly owned, the insurance may provide less of a benefit to the family than anticipated, as estate taxes may consume a significant portion of the death benefit. Why is this so? Because life insurance is typically purchased with the insured also owing the policy, upon the insured's death *the entire death proceeds* are included as part of the insured's taxable estate.

> **Example:** Kyle, a divorced 45-year-old New York resident with two children, has a high-powered job on Wall Street. To ensure that his kids are adequately provided for if he dies prematurely, Kyle purchases a $4 million term life insurance policy on his life and takes ownership of the policy in his own name. Kyle has other assets totaling $5 million. Because Kyle is the owner of the policy, upon his death he will have a total taxable estate of $9 million. If he died in 2022 with the then existing $6,110,000 New York estate tax exemption, the New York estate taxes could be as much as ***$916,400.***

Is this situation avoidable? Absolutely! If in our example Kyle's life insurance had been owned in a properly structured and administered *Irrevocable Life Insurance Trust* (commonly referred to as an ILIT), *none* of the death benefit would have been included as part of the man's taxable estate. The *entire* $9 million would pass to his children free of federal or New York state estate taxes.

An ILIT can provide many other benefits besides estate tax protection. Upon the death of an insured, the insurance proceeds owned in an ILIT can be held in one or more creditor-protected trusts for the benefit of a spouse, children, and other generations. ILIT's can also be used effectively to create "Dynasty Trusts" that can hold assets in trust for multiple generations free of both estate and generation-skipping taxes.

ILIT's can be set up for individuals or couples. For married couples with large estates, it is common to purchase a "second-to-die" life insurance policy that pays out the insurance benefits only upon the death of both the husband and wife. These policies are typically used to provide liquidity to cover estate taxes that may be incurred upon the death of the second spouse. Because the insurance covers two lives, it is usually substantially cheaper than a single life policy, and may often be acquired even if one spouse has health issues.

One caveat: if existing policies are transferred to an ILIT, the insured must live at least three years from the date of transfer to have the death proceeds excluded from his or her taxable estate. If possible, it is best to replace existing policies with new policies owned from the outset by the ILIT trustee; under this arrangement, the death proceeds will be fully excludable from the insured's estate from day one.

Life Insurance With Long-Term Care Access: Covering All the Bases

Most people think about long-term care insurance—if they think about it at all—once they reach their sixties' or beyond. Unfortunately, by that age the cost may seem prohibitive to many of those interested in purchasing the product, or health conditions may render an applicant uninsurable. And frankly, most people believe the need for long-term care will only apply "to the other guy." So, the reasoning goes, "if I don't use the insurance, then all of my premium payments will be 'wasted.'"

According to data from the U.S. Department of Health and Human Services, however, approximately 70 percent of all people 65 years of age or older will need at least some form of long-term care.[18] With the costs for care increasing by leaps and bounds—in my region of New York, the cost for in-home care in 2022 was approximately $275 per day, and nursing home care was at least $375 per day—very few people have enough resources to cover the costs for any extended period. And, with governmental budgets shrinking, Medicaid likely will not continue to be available to cover a large chunk of long-term care costs for the ever-growing baby boomer population.

A possible solution for those reluctant to buy long-term care insurance is the availability of a growing number of "hybrid" life insurance policies that provide lifetime access to the death benefit to cover long-term health care costs. These hybrid policies have been gaining in popularity, with sales doubling between 2008 and 2015 to over $2.4 billion.[19] In 2018, sales of hybrid policies

---

[18] http://longtermcare.gov/the-basics/how-much-care-will-you-need/

[19] http://www.nytimes.com/2016/03/06/business/retirementspecial/hybrid-long-term-care-policies-provide-cash-and-leave-some-behind.html?_r=0

represented 27 percent of the total United States individual life insurance market.[20]

A hybrid policy generally works like this: the policy provides a fixed death benefit and includes a chronic illness rider. Should the insured become disabled— typically defined as suffering from cognitive impairment or needing assistance with two or more "activities of daily living" such as dressing, bathing, toileting, transferring or eating—then the death benefit can be "accelerated" with payments typically of two percent of the death benefit per month to cover long-term care costs. A hybrid policy with a $500,000 death benefit, for example, would provide up to $10,000 per month for 50 months for long-term care needs. If long-term care is not needed, the remaining death benefit would be paid to the surviving spouse or other heirs.

A potential downside is that ownership of a life insurance policy in your individual name is that any cash value built-up in the policy will count as an "available resource" for Medicaid purposes. One strategy to minimize the likelihood that the life insurance will affect the ability of the insured to qualify for Medicaid is to utilize a *Special Needs Irrevocable Life Insurance Trust* established by the insured's children to own the policy. The parent would make cash gifts to the children, who would use the cash to pay the premiums for the life insurance policy owned by the trust. Should the insured require financial assistance to pay for long-term care, the accelerated benefit can be triggered, with the trustee (usually the children) having discretion to use the benefits to contribute towards the parent's long-term care needs. If the parent is Medicaid-eligible, the children would not be forced to distribute money from the

---

[20] Analysts: LTC Hybrid Policies Will Keep Driving Life Insurance Sales - InsuranceNewsNet

insurance policy to cover the parent's long-term care costs, and the death benefit can remain intact. Adding icing on the cake, since the parent has no retained ownership interest in the policy, the death benefit would not be included as part of the parent's taxable estate.

Life Settlements: Maximizing the Value of a Life Insurance Policy During Your Lifetime

People buy life insurance for income replacement, as part of a business buy-sell agreement, for estate tax protection, and for many other reasons. When circumstances change, however, a policy may no longer be needed. For people who own a term insurance policy, the policy is generally allowed to lapse. But for those with "permanent" insurance such as whole life or universal policies, the unneeded policies are often surrendered to the insurance carrier in exchange for its cash value.

But cashing in a policy for its cash value may not be the optimal decision. Given the right set of facts, there may be a better option: the *Life Settlement*.

A Life Settlement is simply the sale of an in-force life insurance party to a third-party purchaser. While most Life Settlements involve the sale of Universal Life or similar "permanent" policies, even some term policies may qualify. Why might a Life Settlement be a better option than surrendering the policy for its cash value? For marketable policies, a Life Settlement will provide a significantly higher payout than surrendering the policy for cash value and will likely have more favorable income tax consequences to boot. The Life Settlement payment will be higher than the cash value because the policy is sold for its fair market value as determined at the time of sale. When a sale is contemplated, the insured's medical information is provided to the company or companies considering making an offer for the policy. If due to his or her declining health the insured is unlikely to live to his or her actuarial life expectancy—but is not terminally ill—the purchasing company will pay more for the policy than merely its cash value. This higher value results because (i) it is likely that the purchaser will collect the death benefit before the insured's actual life expectancy, (ii) the purchaser will have to continue paying the premiums for fewer years, and (iii) there will likely be other proposed purchasers competing for the right to purchase the policy, driving up the price.

In contrast, the cash surrender value for the policy will be lower—often substantially lower—because that value is based on medical underwriting established at the time the policy was written, often years if not decades prior to the proposed sale.

A 2011 study prepared by the research firm Conning & Co. found that of the $500 billion in life insurance policies owned by senior citizens, $100 billion was eligible for life settlements. That same study found that the average life settlement value is 20 percent of the policy's face value, compared with a typical cash value of 10 percent of the face value. So, a life settlement for a life insurance policy with a face value of $1 million would typically net the policyholder $200,000, versus $100,000 if the policy were surrendered for only its cash value.

If this is such a good deal, why haven't you heard about this before? For one thing, Life Settlements are a fairly new planning strategy, and the concept is just gaining traction. In addition, purchasing companies will only be interested in policies with a minimum death benefit of $250,000, and the average value of a policy sold in the present marketplace has a death benefit of $1,800,000.

Know that for someone looking to receive life benefits from a life insurance policy without giving up the death benefit, there may be other options. For example, a policyholder can typically borrow against the cash value in the policy. Also, certain policies contain an option to receive an accelerated death benefit if the insured suffers from a long-term, catastrophic, or terminal illness.

However, if there is a large policy with an insured with some health concerns but is not terminally ill, a Life Settlement is well worth exploring.

"Stranger-Owned" Life Insurance

Over the past three decades seniors nationwide have been targeted with a sales pitch for what is commonly referred to as "stranger-owned" life insurance (STOLI). STOLI is commonly pitched this way: the salesperson tells you that all you need to do is apply for a new life insurance policy insuring your own life. They often recommend a policy with a face amount of a million dollars or more. The policy will cost you nothing, as a third-party lender will provide you with no-risk financing to cover the premium payments. You will retain ownership of the policy for a short term, typically about two years. If you die within the two-year period, your beneficiaries will receive the entire death benefit, less the amount needed to pay off the loan used to fund the insurance premiums. If you survive the two-year window, then you will agree to sell the policy as an "investor." In return, you will receive funds to pay off the loan, commissions, and you will get to keep the extra cash as a profit.

While the STOLI concept seems like a great deal on its face, it is not a legal or legitimate transaction. To obtain life insurance on the life of another person, you must have an "insurable interest" on the life of the insured. Spouses, children, employers, or business partners can have an insurable interest. "Strangers" simply do not fall into the class of persons who would have a legitimate insurable interest in your life. Purchasing life insurance for yourself, with a prearranged agreement to sell the policy would almost certainly be insurance fraud under the laws of any state. Participation in such a transaction can leave you exposed to both civil and criminal liability.

Even if STOLI were a legitimate concept, there are other practical issues that should cause one to avoid these transactions. Foremost, the ultimate owner of the policy will benefit from your "premature" death. Remember that for every year you live, a premium payment must be paid, and the investor's "rate of return" diminishes. Also, the policy may be sold by the original investor (and re-sold multiple times). Do you really want a total stranger benefiting from your premature death?

There are other negative aspects to STOLIs to be considered. The amount of death benefit that a person may have on his or her life at a given time is limited, and if a large STOLI policy is put into place, you might be precluded from obtaining additional insurance that would benefit your family. If you receive any monetary benefits because of the STOLI transaction, those benefits may be taxable income to you. Also, the investors are not bound to purchase the policy at the end of the two-year term, forcing you to pay off the bank loan and begin paying the premiums yourself, or surrender the policy to the bank and possibly causing the IRS to count the discharged debt as taxable income. Such a scenario might leave you owing hundreds of thousands of dollars to the original lender, including interest charges and brokerage fees, and you may not have enough cash to cover the loan.

The STOLI concept has been under attack by various state regulators, beginning in late 2005 when the New York State Insurance Department issued an opinion of its General Counsel holding that STOLI violated New York's insurable interest laws. Other states have since followed suit, and reputable life insurance companies will not participate in true STOLI-type arrangements.

Remember that STOLI should *not* be confused with the life settlement market discussed in the prior section of this chapter. In a life settlement, a policy owner who initially took out a life insurance policy for family or business reasons may later determine that the insurance is no longer needed. In such cases, the policyholder can legally sell the policy to one of several companies that specialize in purchasing such policies on the open market. A life settlement is a legitimate planning tool, while STOLI is an illegitimate scheme in every respect.

Chapter 13 - Basic Asset Protection Strategies

Techniques to Protect <u>Your</u> Assets

When people today think about asset protection, they are most often concerned about protecting assets from the high cost of long-term care. In Part V, I discuss several strategies to protect assets from depletion in a long-term care situation. However, there is an entire universe of risk outside the realm of long-term care planning—car accidents caused by negligence, other torts, malpractice actions, financial setbacks—that require consideration of asset protection strategies.

Different strategies afford different levels of asset protection. Here are some of the most common planning mechanisms:

1. **<u>Tenancy by the Entirety</u>**

This is a type of joint ownership with rights of survivorship available only to married couples. In New York, only real estate may be owned as tenants-by-the-entirety; in some other states, personal property may be owned in this manner. When property is owned as *tenants by the entirety*, a creditor of one spouse may *not* foreclose on the real estate owned by both spouses as *tenants by the entirety*. A drawback of this strategy is that if the non-judgment debtor spouse should die, or if the couple should divorce, the asset protection is lost, and the judgment creditor may be able to seize or foreclose upon the asset.

2. **<u>Corporations</u>**

A corporation allows one or more individuals to own property in a protective form deemed separate from the individual's personal assets. If the corporation incurs a liability, the individual shareholder's personal assets are protected. A disadvantage of a corporation is that if a shareholder had a *personal* judgment creditor, the creditor might seize the majority shareholder's stock. This scenario would prove especially problematic if the shareholder had a majority stake in the corporation, as the shareholder's creditor could gain control of the corporation and its assets.

3. **Limited Partnerships and Limited Liability Companies (LLCs)**

These entities allow for the partners (called "members" in an LLC) to invest in businesses or real estate while receiving protection from any liabilities associated with the entity's assets. Limited partnerships have two types of partners: general partners, with full management control but also unlimited liability for the partnership's debts and obligations; and limited partners, who possess no management authority but have no personal liability towards the company's debts and obligations. LLCs are like limited partnerships, except that no individual member – including those with managerial authority – retains personal liability for the debts or obligations of the LLC.

Due to "charging order" protection, a judgment against a limited partner or a member in an LLC personally will generally *not* allow the judgment creditor to seize the partner's partnership interest or membership interest. Most new business entities today are established as LLCs, since the corporate form does not provide charging order protection.

4. **Domestic Asset Protection Trusts (DAPTs)**

Under common law, a person could not establish a trust in which they could remain a beneficiary and yet have the assets in the trust sheltered from the trust creator's creditors. With Alaska and Delaware leading the way in 1997, there are now 17 states that have passed legislation allowing a person to establish a domestic asset protection trust. Essentially, these are irrevocable trusts in which the grantor can remain a beneficiary and yet have the assets owned in the trust be deemed exempt from any creditor claims against the grantor. They may have the additional bonus of allowing the assets funded into the trust to be lifetime gifts, with the appreciation excluded from the trustmaker's taxable estate. A potential disadvantage of DAPTs is there have been no reported cases testing whether a judgment obtained in one state (e.g., New York) can be enforced against a DAPT created in another state (e.g., Alaska or Delaware) under the "Full Faith and Credit" clause of the U.S. Constitution.

5. **Offshore Asset Protection Trusts (OAPTs)**

These are like DAPT's, but because they are created in foreign jurisdictions such as the Cook Islands, Bermuda, the Bahamas, and other similar jurisdictions, OAPTs not subject to the Full Faith and Credit clause of the U.S. Constitution; accordingly, they are widely considered to provide a higher level of asset protection than a DAPT. In addition, foreign nations typically impose more stringent burdens of proof, shorter statutes of limitation and other legal hurdles that discourage a judgment creditor from pursuing their claim (and will often lead to a settlement more favorable to the judgment debtor). A disadvantage of OAPTs is their higher cost to create and maintain, and the discomfort some people have of dealing with a foreign jurisdiction.

To engage in asset protection planning, you must do so while the "waters are calm." That is, if you already have a judgment against you or know of a potential liability or lawsuit, it may be too late to engage in protective planning. See Chapter 21 for a more in-depth discussion of DAPT's and OAPT's.

6. Trusts to Protect Your Loved Ones' Inheritances

In the prior section I discussed the most common methods for protecting your assets during your lifetime. All too often, however, significant assets passing to the next generation at death are squandered, sometimes as the result of poor spending or investment decisions by the beneficiaries. An oft-cited 2005 study of more than 3,000 wealthy families found that 70 percent of wealthy families lose their wealth by the second generation, and 90 percent lose it by the third generation.[21] In many other cases, however, some or all an inheritance is lost because a beneficiary's creditors swoop in to take a portion of the inheritance before it ever gets to the beneficiary.

Many people know that if they run into financial difficulty, whether it be from losing a job, an illness, a divorce, bad investments, or other life-altering event, their personally owned assets are not protected from their creditors. Assets within the reach of creditors *include* any assets that the person had inherited as an "outright" distribution from the estate of a parent, a spouse, a family member, or any other person.

As I counsel clients during the estate planning process, they often cringe when they learn that, after their death, the assets they have spent a lifetime accumulating and preserving could be lost or squandered if they leave their assets to their loved ones in the form of an outright distribution. It need not be that way. Under New York law, a person can create an estate plan that provides "protective trusts" for the benefit of his or her spouse, children, or other loved ones. The assets left in protective trusts are generally *exempt from the claims of the beneficiaries' creditors.*

---

[21] https://money.com/rich-families-lose-wealth/

In many states protective trusts can allow the beneficiary to serve as his or her own trustee. The trust can also be drafted to provide the beneficiary with sole and absolute discretion to make distributions of income or principal to themselves, in any amounts, at any time. This flexibility gives the beneficiary free access to the assets in the trust. Even with such liberal language, New York law provides that no creditor of the beneficiary can compel the distribution of any of the trust assets to satisfy the creditor's judgment or other claim against the trust beneficiary.

At this point you may be asking, "so, you're telling me that I can leave my spouse or my kids all my assets in a trust that will grant them significant access and control, but will protect those assets from my loved ones' creditors if they ever get sued, and can even shield those assets from a vengeful ex-spouse should they ever divorce?"

Yes, that is what I'm telling you!

The public policy rationale behind these amazing protections is this: when a person makes either a lifetime or after-death gift in trust to another person, the donor has full authority to designate exactly *who* has rights and privileges to the assets in the trust. The trust assets are never "owned" by the beneficiary of the trust; therefore, they are deemed "unavailable" to satisfy the claims of the beneficiary's creditors.

Few other states offer the extensive protective benefits found in New York's law. While the laws of all states provide some form of "spendthrift" creditor protection of assets held in trust, most state laws would not protect trust assets if the beneficiary were the sole trustee and has full discretion to make trust distributions to him or herself. To provide creditor protection, the trust would typically require at least one additional co-trustee to serve with the beneficiary and might require that trust distributions be limited to "health, education, maintenance and support," to afford the creditor protection. Even that standard is not too restrictive, since "maintenance" is interpreted to allow the use of trust assets to maintain the beneficiary's standard of living. Such "maintenance" could include cars, houses, vacations, tickets to the theater–the list is almost without practical limitation.

In cases where there is a minor or disabled child, a child who has financial or addiction issues, or simply where the parent wishes to place greater controls on the disposition of trust assets, a trust administered by a third-party trustee may well be appropriate. But in a significant majority of cases, establishing a beneficiary-controlled trust will be the appropriate planning tool to ensure that only the beneficiary and, if applicable, your other descendants, will benefit from the assets you've worked hard to acquire and preserve over your lifetime.

Under the law of 33 states and the District of Columbia you cannot establish a spendthrift trust for *yourself* and retain access to the assets while protecting the assets from your own creditors. However, as discussed in Chapter 21, 17 states have adopted some form of Domestic Asset Protection Trust legislation that authorize creation and funding of self-settled spendthrift trusts.

PART V: PLANNING FOR DISABILITY - LONG-TERM CARE & MEDICAID PLANNING

Chapter 14 - The Importance of Planning for Incapacity

People often think of estate planning only in the context of "death planning." However, failing to account for the possibility that someday you may need help managing your personal and financial affairs might prove to be a huge mistake. If no one is vested with authority to handle your affairs in the event of your incapacity, your loved one might be forced to file a court petition for *guardianship*. Guardianships are time consuming, expensive, require the involvement of multiple attorneys, and are cumbersome, as court-appointed guardians must file annual accountings with the court and are subject to ongoing court supervision.

One major advantage of a living trust as compared with a last will and testament is that a will is effective only upon the testator's death and is of no value if the testator becomes disabled during his or her lifetime. In contrast, a living trust is a contractual agreement that becomes effective as soon as it is executed and funded with the client's assets. The trust will typically provide that one or more *successor trustees* are authorized and directed to administer the trustmaker's financial and personal affairs in the event of the trustmaker's disability. Note that the successor trustees have control over only those assets owned by the living trust, highlighting the importance of transferring (or "funding) the trustmaker's assets to the trust during his or her lifetime.

An important consideration in a living trust design is the mechanism for determining *when* the trustmaker is in fact disabled. Many "boilerplate" trust documents provide that the trustmaker is deemed disabled when a doctor, or maybe two doctors, make such a determination. Given the option, however, many people prefer having their spouse, adult children, or other loved ones participate in such a critical determination. A living trust can include a *disability panel* composed of one or more medical professionals and a combination of family members or friends. The disability panel may be given authority to determine the trustmaker's disability by unanimous vote, by a majority, or any other method as determined by the trustmaker.

Once the disability panel has decided that the trustmaker is disabled, the successor trustees will be authorized by the terms of the trust to take control of the trustmaker's personal and financial affairs. Many trusts will provide that the successor trustees are to simply provide for the trustmaker's "general welfare," or similar words. Such an open-ended approach gives the successor trustees little guidance and gives little insight into the trustmaker's true feelings. Also, such generic language gives the successor trustees no authority to use trust assets to provide for the well-being of the trustmaker's spouse, children, or other beneficiaries.

Living trusts can be drafted to provide the successor trustees with detailed disability instructions customized to meet the trustmaker's goals and objectives. Such provisions might include the trustmaker's preference for living arrangements, their favorite hobbies and activities, preference for religious or spiritual practices, instructions regarding the care of pets, and a description of other beneficiaries whom the trustees may provide for out of the trust assets.

If a living trust is not utilized, the typical tool used to address the client's possible lifetime disability issues is a statutory general durable power of attorney (POA). A POA typically grants one or more designated "agents" the authority to handle personal and financial affairs of the "principal" who has signed the POA.

In 2009 New York significantly revised its statutory "short form" power of attorney form. Attorneys and the public found the form, which required use of a separate rider to authorize gifting powers for the agents, to be overly complicated and too easily rejected by financial institutions and other third parties.

After years of intense lobbying by New York estate planning and elder law attorneys and with other interested constituencies, the New York legislature passed a significant revision to the New York power of attorney statute that was signed into law on December 15, 2020, with the new statutory short form going into effect on June 13, 2021.

One significant change from the prior form is that the statutory gifts rider (SGR) is no longer required to enable the principal to authorize the agent under the instrument to make gifts of the principal's assets. Under the 2020 statute all gifting provisions are included under the "Modifications" section of the single form. Gifting powers are useful in many contexts but are essential in Medicaid planning where most of the principal's assets must be transferred to a spouse or children to maximize asset preservation when the principal requires long-term care. All too often I meet with family members whose now incapacitated spouse or parent has a POA executed under the prior law that does not include the SGR, and the principal no longer has the requisite mental capacity to sign a new POA that includes gifting powers. In that case the family may have no other choice but to file a time consuming and expensive guardianship proceeding to obtain judicial approval to make gifts of the principal's assets for Medicaid planning purposes.

Another major improvement in the new law is that no longer can a financial institution or other third party be permitted to reject a POA for failure to comply with the "exact wording" of the statutory form. Under the prior law financial institutions often rejected a POA for all types of incidental deviations from the statutory form, even something so inconsequential as a missing comma or period. The new statute requires only that the POA "substantially conforms" to the wording of the statutory form to be deemed a valid statutory short form POA.

Attorneys often face the difficult dilemma where the client cannot sign the POA due to a physical limitation. The new law will allow for a third party to sign the instrument at the direction of the disabled principal.

One frequent criticism of the prior POA statute was that there were no financial damages that could be assessed against a third party that refused to accept a properly executed POA. The sole remedy for an aggrieved party who was compelled to sue the recalcitrant financial institution or other third party was to obtain a court order for the rejecting party to accept the POA, leaving the injured party on the hook for their own attorneys' fees and court costs. Under the new law most third parties who reject a POA absent "Reasonable Cause" as defined in the statute --there are exceptions for many government agencies and similar institutions-- may be required to pay the injured party financial damages along with reasonable attorneys' fees and costs. This enhanced legal remedy should serve as a significant deterrent against third parties rejecting a POA without adequate justification.

In recognition of the legitimate concerns that elderly people are often targeted for fraud, the new POA form must be notarized and witnessed by two witnesses, one of whom can also be the notary. The prior POA statute required only that the document be notarized, but in cases where the SGR was used, that rider had to be notarized and witnessed by two witnesses, which contributed to the complexity of signing a fully functional POA under the prior statutory form.

The new POA form will be a game changer in simplifying the management of financial matters for many people, especially seniors who wish to delegate financial decision-making authority to their spouse or children. And with gifting powers to now be included in the same instrument as other delegated powers, attorneys ought to regularly incorporate gift giving authority in POA's should the principal later need long-term care. Including broad gifting powers in a POA allows the named agent(s) to quickly transfer the principal's assets to a spouse or children as part of a comprehensive asset protection plan.

A POA can be drafted with "springing" powers that will be effective only upon the happening of a future event, typically certification by the principal's physician that the principal has become incapacitated. In most cases, however, clients choose to have the POA immediately effective upon signing. While the immediately effective POA is easy to use by the agent, it's subject to abuse if the agent is unscrupulous.

But even when a POA is not abused by the agent, there is another significant flaw in relying upon the POA as the sole source of disability planning. While a typical "immediately effective" POA authorizes a third-party agent to handle the principal's financial affairs, there is no mechanism in the POA to "take away" the principal's power to inflict financial harm on himself.

> **Example:** I received a call from "Artie." Artie's mother "Doris" was in her early 80's and had progressive dementia. Artie was Doris's only child and was named agent under Doris's POA.
>
> Artie, who lived on the west coast, was contacted by a manager at Doris's bank who told Artie that Doris was making frequent large withdrawals from her bank account. Artie did a little digging and discovered that his mother had been conned into believing she had won a multi-million-dollar

sweepstakes, but to claim her "winnings" she had to pay "taxes and fees" in advance.

Artie retained me to file for guardianship under Article 81 of the Mental Hygiene Law. Although we were able to have Doris's accounts quickly frozen, by that time she had already given the scammers over $157,000.

Artie's situation likely would not have been so dire had his mother's estate plan included a revocable or irrevocable living trust with disability planning provisions. A living trust could have provided that if Doris was deemed disabled upon a determination by her disability panel, Artie would be designated as "disability trustee" for the administration of the trust and its assets. By naming trusted people while the trustmaker is of "sound mind," the trustmaker creates a protective mechanism to ensure that at some future time a successor trustee is available to take over control of the trustmaker's personal and financial affairs, even if the trustmaker—as was apparently the case with Artie's mother—believes she is "fine." A POA is not designed to facilitate this same seamless transfer of authority and responsibility, sometimes necessitating costly, stressful, and unpredictable court guardianship proceedings.

Chapter 15 - Proactive Planning for Long-Term Care: The Medicaid Asset Protection Trust

As discussed in Chapters 16 and 17, planning for the possibility you may need long-term care involves navigating among a dizzying array of federal, state, and local laws and regulations. While a skilled elder law attorney can help families preserve significant assets by utilizing various crisis-planning techniques, it is always better to act proactively by planning well before any care may be needed. If long-term care insurance is not an option, a *Medicaid Asset Protection Trust*, or "MAPT," is an extraordinary asset protection tool.

Long-term care is paid for from three primary sources: (i) the person's own assets; (ii) long-term care insurance; or (iii) the Medicaid program. In 2022, a person does not qualify for nursing home Medicaid coverage in New York until they have "countable resources" of not more than $16,800. While a person may choose to "spend down" their assets to qualify for Medicaid, most people prefer to preserve as much of their assets as possible for themselves and their heirs.

The problem with waiting too late to protect your assets is that most asset transfers made within five years of applying for nursing home Medicaid coverage, excluding a transfer to a spouse or a disabled child, results in a period of Medicaid ineligibility. In 2022 in New York's Hudson Valley region, a non-exempt transfer of $200,000 of assets made during the five-year "look-back period" would disqualify an "otherwise eligible" person—meaning a person with $16,800 of assets or less at the time of application—from receiving nursing home Medicaid coverage for about 14.9 months. Understandably, a nursing home will not be keen on letting a person reside in the facility for any period without paying for their care. Since Medicaid will not initially pick up the tab, the facility will almost certainly seek payment from the resident—or the family members to whom the assets were transferred during the look-back period—and often will sue if payment is not made to cover the cost of care.

Proactive planning—that is, engaging in asset preservation techniques at least five years before long-term care is likely needed—is the best way to preserve as many of one's assets as possible. The most effective way to maximize the amount of assets that can be protected from a Medicaid "spenddown" is to make a "gift with strings attached" by creating and funding assets into a MAPT.

A MAPT is simply a particular type of irrevocable trust. Why irrevocable? The garden variety revocable trust is not an effective asset protection vehicle; since the trustmaker has full access to the assets, under Medicaid rules the assets in a revocable trust are deemed "available" to the trustmaker and must be "spent down" before the trustmaker becomes eligible for Medicaid coverage.

Figure 2 shows the structure of a typical MAPT that provides income-only to the trustmaker and authorizes discretionary principal distributions to a class of beneficiaries (often descendants) during the trustmaker's lifetime:

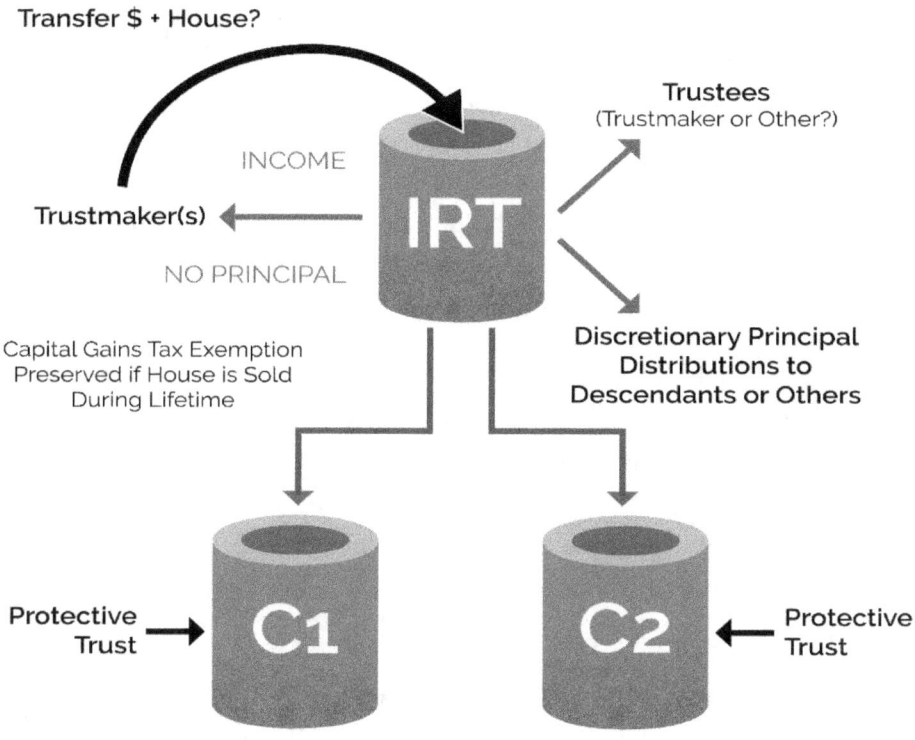

Figure 2. The Medicaid Asset Protection Trust

Transfers of assets to a properly structured MAPT, however, will be deemed a "transfer" of assets for Medicaid purposes as of the date the assets are funded into the trust. This feature is important, because for effective Medicaid planning, we want to "start the clock" for the five-year look-back period sooner rather than later. The sooner the clock begins to run, the sooner we get through the five-year look-back period, thereby protecting all the trust assets, as well any appreciation of those assets, should the trustmaker later need long-term care.

A significant advantage of the MAPT over outright gifts to children is that, as shown in Figure 2, the parent can retain all the income from the trust, with the income taxed to the parent rather than the child, often at a lower income tax rate. For clients who have no intention to use the principal but need the income, this feature holds great appeal. Also, the trust structure also ensures that the trustmaker has effectively made a gift "with strings attached." The parent can retain control over the trust operation by serving as trustee, and can even retain the power to change the ultimate trust beneficiaries, with a parent retaining authority to disinherit a child and give their share to a grandchild, another child, etc.

Another benefit of the MAPT is the ability to avoid capital gains taxes upon the beneficiary's ultimate sale of the assets. So long as the MAPT is properly structured as a complete "grantor" trust, and as long as the assets are held in the trust until the parent's death, those assets will receive a "step-up" in cost basis. That is, the assets will be revalued for income tax purposes using the date of death value.

> **Example:** if a share of stock with an original cost basis of $10 is given outright to a child and then sold for $100, the child will have a taxable gain of $90. If the same stock is placed in the MAPT and held until death with a date of death value of $100, the same sale will produce no taxable gain.

Transferring a primary residence to a MAPT retains the step-up in basis advantage and provides the further benefit that the trustmaker retains (i) a lifetime right to remain in the residence and (ii) all the property tax exemptions they may already have. In addition, should the house be sold during the trustmaker's lifetime, the trustmaker will remain eligible for the capital gains tax exemption exclusively available to home sellers ($250,000 exemption for an individual seller, $500,000 for a married couple).

For all the benefits afforded by the MAPT, however, people are often understandably hesitant to do something "irrevocably." No matter how much income they have, they often ask, "but what if I really need to access the principal in the trust?" Or there always remains the concern regarding a possible need for nursing home care within five years of funding the assets to the trust, which results in the trust assets being deemed "countable resources" for Medicaid purposes.

Fortunately, the laws of many states, including New York law, provide a simple method of revoking even an irrevocable trust. Revoking a trust created under New York law simply requires the written consent of the trustmaker and all the trust beneficiaries.[22] Once the trust is revoked, the trust assets can be returned to the trustmaker, effectively "undoing" the property transfers. Although there may be gift tax consequences for a revocation, this is rarely an issue as very few estates in which a MAPT is used are large enough to require the payment of gift taxes.

A practical problem arises, however, when the trust includes minor beneficiaries, often the trustmaker's grandchildren. Revocation under Estates, Powers and Trusts Law §7-1.9 cannot be utilized with minor beneficiaries, since they are legally prohibited from consenting to a revocation. Fortunately, there is an easy fix for this problem. The trustmaker may retain a lifetime "power of appointment" to remove or add additional principal beneficiaries during the trustmaker's lifetime. Should the need arise to terminate a trust, the trustmaker can simply exercise the power of appointment to eliminate the minor beneficiaries from the trust, after which the trust can be revoked by the trustmaker and the adult beneficiaries.

Another possible hurdle is the circumstance where a trust revocation is necessary because the trustmaker has a sudden health

---

[22] Estates, Powers & Trusts Law § 7-1.9(a)

crisis (such as a stroke), but the trustmaker is incapable of consenting to the revocation. This problem is easily solved by including in both the trust and in the trustmaker's durable power of attorney a provision authorizing the agent under the power of attorney to terminate any trusts created by the trustmaker. This technique was approved in a 2012 New York court case that held that a trustmaker may authorize an attorney-in-fact designated under the trustmaker's power of attorney to act under EPTL §7-1.9 to amend or revoke the trustmaker's irrevocable trust under, so long as the power of attorney grants the attorney-in-fact the power broad general authority to act.[23]

By virtue of New York's powerful revocation powers, using a MAPT provides seniors with a wonderful vehicle of protecting selected assets, while retaining the right to income from the assets, and significant control over the disposition of the trust principal. Note that other states may not permit all the MAPT techniques allowed in New York, so it is imperative to obtain counsel from an elder law attorney in your jurisdiction to see if a MAPT is suitable for your situation.

What About a Deed with a Retained Life Estate?

For elder law attorneys one of the most requested legal services is for preparing a deed transferring a parents' home to their children, with the parents reserving a *life estate* interest in the home. The general purpose of such an arrangement—often called a "life estate deed"—is to protect the home if the parents someday need long-term care assistance and hope to qualify for Medicaid coverage. However, under virtually any scenario, transferring a home to a

---

[23] Perosi v. LiGreci, 98 A.D.3d 230, 948 N.Y.S.2d 629 (2012)

MAPT described previously in this chapter is a better option than using a life estate deed.

If successfully implemented, both the life estate deed and the MAPT will protect a primary residence if the homeowner does not apply for Medicaid long-term care coverage for at least five years from the date the strategy is implemented. But the MAPT has several significant advantages over the life estate deed that makes the MAPT the strategy of choice. Here are some of the key differences:

- If the home is sold after being conveyed to the MAPT, the entire capital gain will qualify for the capital gain exemption that is available only to owners of a primary residence ($250,000 exemption for individuals, $500,000 for married couples). By contrast, if the home is sold after being conveyed with a life estate deed, the portion of the home transferred to the children as "remainder beneficiaries" will be subject to capital gains tax.

    Example: Assume that a 75-year-old widow executes a life estate deed transferring the remainder interest in her home to her children and the house is sold during the mother's lifetime. Assuming a current interest rate of 2.6 percent, if the capital gain from the sale were to equal $200,000, the children would be liable for a capital gain tax on the approximately 76 percent of the sale price attributed to the children's remainder interest under the IRS's Table "S" used in New York State for life expectancy calculations. If the capital gains tax rate were 25 percent, the children would owe a capital gains tax of approximately $38,000 upon the sale.

- A transfer to children using a life estate deed is typically an irrevocable transfer. If, for example, a parent later has a falling-out with a child, the parent cannot "undo" that transfer. A flexibly structured MAPT will include a *limited power of appointment* that permits the parent to change the trust beneficiaries during the parent's lifetime and retains for the parent the right to decide who receives the trust assets after the time of the parent's death.

- If a parent enters a nursing home and the children elect to sell the parent's residence, under the life estate deed technique Medicaid will be entitled to reimbursement for the portion of the sale proceeds equal to the value of the parent's remaining life estate interest at the time of sale. So, even after expiration of the five-year look-back period, if a 75-year-old in a nursing home is on Medicaid and their home is sold for $250,000, Medicaid will be entitled to reimbursement for the parent's approximately 26 percent portion of the sale proceeds (or $65,000). In contrast, there is no Medicaid reimbursement requirement if a residence held by a MAPT is sold while the parent is receiving Medicaid assistance.

Chapter 16 - Long-Term Care: How Will I Pay the Cost?

Since 1980, the percentage of Americans 65 and older has increased from 11 percent to 16 percent of the population, with over 55 million Americans being 65 or older as of the 2020 census.[24] By 2060, it is estimated that 98 million Americans—almost 22 percent of the population—will be 65 or older.[25]

With an aging population comes the increasing demand for long-term care services. Long-term care is generally defined as the provision of services to assist with "activities of daily living" such as: bathing, dressing, toileting, transferring to or from a bed or chair, meal preparation, eating, housework, managing money, taking medication, and shopping.[26]

When given the choice, most people would prefer to "age in place" in their residence rather than in a nursing home or similar facility. But for everyone other than the wealthy, paying the cost for long-term care is a major stumbling block.

One possible solution is long-term care insurance (LTCI). Over the past few decades approximately eight million Americans have purchased LTCI[27] to provide coverage towards the ever-increasing costs of long-term care. A prevailing fear is that the cost of long-term care can wipe out a lifetime of savings. This fear is not unfounded, as today in my home county of Orange County, New

---

[24] Source: https://usafacts.org/state-of-the-union/population

[25] Source: U.S. Department of Health and Human Services

[26] Source: longtermcare.gov/the-basics/what is long-term-care/

[27] Source: American Association for Long-Term Care Insurance

York, the cost of a private room in a nursing home can run over $500 *per day*.

Often LTCI policies were sold with the promise that the premiums would not increase. In the past few years, however, the LTCI industry has been in turmoil, as many insurance companies have stopped issuing LTCI policies altogether, and the dwindling few that remain have dramatically raised the cost of premiums for existing policyholders.

For example, in January 2016, Genworth's LTCI policyholders in New York received notice of a stunning 60 percent increase in the cost of premiums for the same coverage. But perhaps we New Yorkers don't have it so bad; according to a 2016 article in *Money*, Genworth petitioned Pennsylvania insurance regulators for permission to raise premiums on some of its policyholders in that state by as much as 130 percent![28]

To reduce the severity of the premium increase, insurers raising rates will typically offer policyholders the option to reduce benefits or otherwise modify their LTCI policies. For example, many existing LTCI policies include a five percent compound inflation benefit, which allows the policies to keep up with rising long-term care costs. To hold down the premium increase, policyholders may go to a three percent compound option, change from a compound interest option to simple interest, or even forgo any inflation coverage. Another option may be to reduce the number of years of maximum coverage; many existing policies provide for five years' worth of protection, which can be reduced to four or even three years. While choosing the alternative options will reduce the size of the premium increase, the policies will provide correspondingly

---

[28] "Why Long-term Care insurance is Becoming a Tougher Call," *Money*, March 8, 2016

fewer benefits than what the policyholder had originally signed up for.

What's the cause of the chaos in the LTCI market? As noted in the *Money* article, when LTCI products were first introduced in the 1970s, insurance companies grossly miscalculated the economic realities of the marketplace, and their actuarial models were wildly inaccurate. Life expectancies have continued to rise, and the cost of long-term care has exceeded the insurance companies' projections. These factors, combined with the low interest rate environment we've experienced since the 2007-08 economic crisis, has severely dampened the insurance companies' earnings on the invested premiums, resulting in the insurance companies suffering massive losses. As but one example, Genworth's CEO told *Money* that his company had lost $2 billion on its LTCI policies and was continuing to lose between $100 million and $150 million per year on the product.

If LTCI is not a viable option, how about Medicare? Unfortunately, Medicare provides minimal coverage for long-term care costs, and only then for "skilled" care such as nursing care, physical therapy, speech therapy and occupational therapy. Medicare provides *limited* coverage for nursing home stays if, and only if, these requirements are satisfied: (i) the patient is hospitalized at least three consecutive days excluding the day of discharge; (ii) the nursing home admission takes place within thirty days of the hospital discharge (with limited exceptions); (iii) the patient requires skilled nursing or skilled rehabilitation services, or both, and such services can be provided only in a skilled nursing facility on an in-patient basis; (iv) the services are provided for a condition treated in the hospital; and (v) the patient's stay is approved by the facility's peer review committee.

Even when a patient obtains Medicare approval for a long-term care stay, Medicare will pay for a *maximum* coverage period of 100 days. Of the 100-day maximum coverage period, only the first 20 days would be covered at 100 percent of the cost; for days 21 through 100, the patient was responsible for a co-pay amount that in 2022 ran a hefty $194.50 per day. Furthermore, the coverage may be revoked anytime during the 100-day coverage period if Medicare determines that the patient no longer requires skilled nursing or rehabilitation care.

For many years nursing homes and home health care providers have routinely terminated Medicare coverage for rehabilitation and related care on the theory that the patient has "ceased to improve" notwithstanding the skilled nursing care provided to the patient. While the patient always had the right to appeal such a determination, many patients, when faced with the legal costs and emotional strain, simply throw in the towel and accede to the decision. After Medicare is terminated because a patient has allegedly flunked the "improvement standard"—and thus no longer remains covered by "skilled" care—the patient is deemed eligible only for custodial care, which as has been noted is not covered under Medicare. In those cases, the patient (if they do not have long-term care insurance) either needs to privately pay for their care or apply for Medicaid if they meet the financial eligibility criteria.

In 2013, however, the federal government settled a class action lawsuit[29] that was filed on behalf of patients affected by this draconian policy. The result is an expansion of the conditions under which Medicare must cover skilled nursing care, which no longer can "turn on the presence or absence of a beneficiary's potential for improvement from therapy, but rather on the beneficiary's need for

---

[29] *Jimmo v. Sebelius,* No. 11-CV-17 (D. Vt.)

skilled care."[30] Medicare must cover skilled nursing care even if the patient's condition were to deteriorate while receiving such care, so long as the care is determined to have slowed such deterioration.

In the years ahead, we may see a significant increase in Medicare funded home care services for patients with chronic conditions such as Alzheimer's, Parkinson's, traumatic brain injuries, and multiple sclerosis. Going forward, patients with these conditions should find greater access to Medicare-covered services such as physical, occupational and speech therapies in their home setting. While the costs to Medicare for such services is almost certain to increase in the near term, we can hope that the greater availability of home-based care will reduce the number of people who need to be placed in nursing homes, where the costs of care are even greater than in the home setting.

---

[30] www.cms.gov/medicare/medicare-fee-for-service-payment/SNFPPS/downloads/jimmo-factsheet.pdf

Chapter 17 - Medicaid For Long-Term Care

Given that relatively few people can cover a significant portion of long-term care expenses with either LTCI or Medicare, the best option for many people is Medicaid. Contrary to popular belief, a person rarely needs to "spend-down" all or even most of their assets to qualify for Medicaid long-term care coverage. This chapter will describe the basics of the Medicaid long-term care program, and various methods for attaining Medicaid eligibility without having to spend virtually every penny *before* being made eligible for Medicaid coverage.

Medicaid Residency Requirements

Medicaid is a mammoth governmental health insurance program governed by a complex web of federal and state statutes, regulations, and administrative directives. As the only public source of funding available to cover a substantial portion of long-term nursing home costs, it is important to understand the residency requirements associated with the Medicaid program.

To receive Medicaid in a state, an applicant must be a resident of that state. Under New York law, there is no durational requirement for a person to establish residency in New York, as confirmed by the New York Court of Appeals in the landmark case of *In Re Shah*[31]. A Medicaid applicant who satisfies the financial eligibility criteria can be a resident of New York for a single day and obtain Medicaid coverage. A person will be deemed a resident of New York if they are living in the state, and they intend to remain in New York "permanently or indefinitely." A New York nursing home resident who cannot express such intent—if, for example, they have dementia—will be deemed a New York resident, except

---

[31] In re Shah, 95 N.Y.2d 148, 733 N.E.2d 1093 (2000)

in the rare circumstance they were placed in a New York facility by another state's social service agency.

Once it is determined that a Medicaid applicant meets the state's residency requirement, the county in which the person resides will be responsible for the Medicaid services provided by the county. When a person has more than one physical residence, factors such as where the applicant is registered to vote, where they receive mail, the address on the applicant's driver's license, and where the applicant's Social Security check is sent are all considered in determining their permanent "home." Establishing the primary residence is important, because elderly persons needing care will frequently move within the state to a long-term care facility closer to a child or other family members. For example, if a Nassau County, New York resident moves directly to an Orange County, New York nursing home, the Medicaid application must be administered through the Nassau County Department of Social Services. If, however, prior to entering the Orange County nursing home, the resident had moved from Nassau County to her daughter's home in Orange County—and truly established residency, evidenced by such actions as changing the address on her driver's license and registering to vote in Orange County—the Medicaid application would be properly filed and administered in Orange County.

If a person enters a New York nursing home and was not previously a New York State resident, then the county where the nursing home is located will be responsible for administering that person's Medicaid application under the "where found" rule.

If there is a dispute between two counties as to which county is responsible for processing a Medicaid application, the county in which the Medicaid applicant is "found" must at least initially process the application and determine the applicant's Medicaid eligibility. If the counties cannot resolve their dispute, the county where the application is submitted must provide the Medicaid benefits—assuming the applicant is eligible—with the "payer" county having the right to request an administrative hearing at the state level to resolve the dispute between the counties. In no event should the otherwise eligible applicant suffer any interruption of Medicaid benefits.

Community Medicaid: An Overview

As of 2022, the maximum amount of "countable resources" a Medicaid applicant may retain will vary between a low of $2,000 and a high of $16,800, depending upon the state of residence. Two general types of Medicaid programs cover long-term care expenses: community-based Medicaid and "institutional" Medicaid that pays for nursing home costs. To obtain Community Medicaid services that assists with the "activities of daily living," an applicant in a "generous" state such as New York can retain the maximum exempt resources permitted under federal law ($16,800 in 2021), plus their home (which is deemed an exempt resource). But removing "excess" resources for Community Medicaid purposes is rather straightforward, as in most states under Community Medicaid there is currently only a one-month "look-back" period for asset transfers to persons other than a spouse; this is in contrast to the nursing home Medicaid program, which currently imposes a period of ineligibility for benefits for most types of asset transfers made to non-spouses during the five-year "look-back" period prior to applying for nursing home Medicaid.

Given that as of the date of this writing there are no asset transfer penalties for spousal transfers for Community Medicaid in New York, the usual strategy in spousal cases is to transfer any excess resources into the name of the "well" spouse. For single applicants, or where both spouses need care, assets can be transferred to other family members, or to trusts for their benefit.

Regarding income requirements, the maximum income allowance for Community Medicaid in 2022 was $934 per month. With no planning, any excess income must be applied to a Medicaid "spend down," with Medicaid then paying the balance towards the cost of care. For example, a person with $2,000 per month of recurring income (typically Social Security and a pension) would have to contribute $1,066 of her income towards her cost of home care, with Medicaid paying the difference.

A practical limitation of the income rules is that the $934 income allowance does not consider the applicant's household expenses, such as rent, mortgage, property taxes, or utilities. Given those typical expenses, it can be difficult if not impossible for most people to live off the monthly Medicaid income allowance after satisfying the spend down requirement.

Fortunately, the Community Medicaid rules permit an applicant of any age to fund their excess income into a vehicle known as a "Pooled Income Trust." Pooled Income Trusts are statutorily approved trusts established and operated by various charitable organizations. To participate in a Pooled Income Trust, the Medicaid applicant signs a "joinder agreement" prepared by the charity that operates the trust. Once Medicaid is approved, the participant's excess income would be transferred to the Pooled Income Trust and held in a separate trust account for the participant's benefit. Each month the participant (or often their representative, such as an agent under a power of attorney) may submit bills incurred by the participant for household expenses such as rent, food, clothing, utilities, etc. The Pooled Income Trust Trustee may pay any such non-medical bills incurred by the participant. If after payment for such expenses the participant has excess income, such income will remain part of the Pooled Income Trust and can be used towards the charitable purposes of the organization administering the Trust.

Many of the commonly used Pooled Income Trusts have initial enrolment fees of $200 to $300, with small monthly administrative fees of either a flat dollar amount (typically around $20 for a certain number of transactions, with extra fees for each additional transaction) or a percentage of the participant's monthly income. Most trusts also have a small annual accounting fee, typically about $50.

Ideally the excess monthly income paid into the Pooled Income Trust should be completely spent on the participant's personal expenses each month, since if there are funds left in the participant's sub-account at their death, those funds cannot be distributed to the participant's heirs but instead will remain with the non-profit that operates the Pooled income Trust to be used for the organization's charitable purposes.

Enrollment in a Pooled Income Trust can often mean the difference-maker in allowing a person to be cared for in their home rather than having to go to a nursing home. The mechanics of incorporating the Pooled Income Trust with a Community Medicaid application can be complex, so before going down this road you should seek the counsel of an elder law attorney experienced in working with Pooled Trusts.

Will We See a Look-Back Period for New York Community Medicaid?

Even before the COVID-19 crisis, New York was facing a $6 billion budget deficit. With the realization that Medicaid expenditures devour approximately one-third of the state budget, in 2019 then Governor Cuomo appointed a "Medicaid Redesign Team" (MRT) to find ways to reduce New York's Medicaid costs.

The MRT ultimately recommended several changes to the New York Medicaid program, several which were included as part of the budget approved in April 2020. Perhaps the biggest change is that for the first time New York may impose a "penalty period" for certain asset transfers made by persons seeking community based long-term care Medicaid services, including care provided in the applicant's home, an adult home, or an assisted living facility.

Under federal law, states must impose a financial penalty when a nursing home Medicaid applicant makes gifts of their assets, with certain limited exceptions. For over a decade there has been in place a five-year look-back period for nursing home Medicaid coverage, with the look-back period beginning as of the date that is five years prior to the date the Medicaid application is filed, but only so long as at the time of filing the Medicaid applicant is "otherwise eligible" for Medicaid; to be "otherwise eligible," the applicant can then have no more than $16,800 in "countable resources" in 2022. Under the rules, a nursing home Medicaid applicant must provide five years of records for all financial accounts owned by the applicant during the look-back period. If there are gifts made during that period to children or other non-spousal recipients (excluding disabled beneficiaries), the rules require imposition of a "penalty period" commensurate with the total value of all non-exempt uncompensated transfers. The penalty period is determined by dividing the total amount of the uncompensated transfers during the look-back by the "Regional Rate," which is the average monthly private pay nursing home cost in each of seven regions in New York State as determined annually by the Department of Health. For 2022, the Regional Rate in the Hudson Valley is $13,399.

If, for example, a nursing home Medicaid applicant from the Hudson Valley has made non-exempt transfers during the five-year look-back period totaling $200,000, the penalty period imposed will be determined by dividing $200,000 by $13,399, resulting in a penalty period of 14.93 months. Assuming the Medicaid applicant is "otherwise eligible" at the time of application, Medicaid coverage would be delayed for 14.93 months, leaving the applicant and her family on the hook for the nursing home bill during the penalty period.

Unlike nursing home Medicaid, states have the option whether to impose look-back and penalty periods for community Medicaid services. New York has been one of a handful of states that has never imposed penalties for persons applying for community Medicaid services. A person seeking community Medicaid benefits in New York can simply transfer to their heirs all their assets in excess of the $16,900 resource allowance and be eligible for Community Medicaid long-term care coverage by the following month.

But that may change. In 2020 New York adopted a 30-month look-back period for Community Medicaid long-term care programs, with all transfers made on or after October 1, 2020, to be subject to the new look-back rules. While the look-back period for Community Medicaid services will be half as long as the penalty for nursing home Medicaid, the penalty for non-exempt transfers made during the 30-month look-back will be determined using the same "Regional Rate" as used for nursing home cases. So, $200,000 in non-exempt transfers made within the new 30-month look-back will result in the same 14.93-month penalty for Community Medicaid services as if the applicant were in a nursing home.

The new rules were to be effective as of October 1, 2020, but due to COVID-19, the presumed effective date was pushed back to January 1, 2021. With COVID-19 persisting into 2022, the effective date was pushed back indefinitely, and the earliest the new rules will be effective is October 2022. To implement this new look-back period, New York State must file a waiver request with the federal Centers for Medicare & Medicaid Services, and as of this writing we have no information that the waiver request has been filed. It is possible New York's waiver request may not be approved, and the Community Medicaid look-back rules will never go into effect.

Even if the 30-month Community Medicaid look-back is ultimately implemented, one bit of good news for New York Medicaid applicants is that the "spousal refusal" rules have been retained in New York. Under spousal refusal, any amount of assets can be transferred between spouses without resulting in a penalty period for either nursing home or community Medicaid programs. Elimination of spousal refusal was on the MRT's chopping block, but because of lobbying by the New York Elder Law & Special Needs Section of the New York State Bar Association and other interested stakeholder, spousal refusal remains a valuable planning tool. But we can expect spousal refusal to continue to be a target for elimination in future years.

Assisted Living & Continuing Care Retirement Communities (CCRC)

While people almost always prefer to stay in their homes as they age, there are sometimes circumstances where that is impractical. All the same, a person who is unable or unwilling to live alone at home often will not need the level of care provided by a nursing home. Fortunately, there is an array of "intermediate" living arrangements that may be appropriate for seniors with different needs and circumstances.

One popular option is the *Continuing Care Retirement Community* (CCRC). A CCRC provides a "tiered" approach to addressing the aging process. A person who can live independently would pay an "entrance fee" that can range from the low six figures to $1 million or more depending upon the facility, the type of apartment unit chosen, and the refund option, if any, selected. People paying the lowest entrance fee would receive none of the fee upon leaving the facility, and nothing would be paid to their heirs upon their death. Those paying the higher buy-in fees would be entitled to a refund upon departure or death, typically ranging from 50 percent to 90 percent. Besides the entrance fee, the resident would also pay a monthly fee typically ranging from three-thousand dollars to six-thousand dollars that usually includes one meal a day and unlimited use of the CCRC's facilities, which may be luxurious.

One key benefit of a CCRC is that if a resident's health declines, the facility offers varied levels of care included as part of the entrance fee and the monthly fee. A person may move from the independently living apartment, then to an assisted living unit, and finally to a nursing home unit, all within the same facility. For married couples, this may be especially appealing since the "well" spouse can stay in the independent living apartment and still remain close to their spouse.

While CCRCs have many benefits, a downside is that Medicaid will cover no portion of the monthly residency fee.

Another type of living arrangement is a traditional Adult Home, also known as an Assisted Living Residence (ALR). ALRs are licensed adult homes or enriched housing units that house five or more adult residents. There are presently over 7,700 licensed ALR beds in New York State.

To meet statutory licensing requirements, ALRs must provide 24-hour on-site monitoring, personal care services and/or home care services, daily meals and snacks, case management services, and an individualized service plan. ALR costs are _not_ covered by Medicaid or Medicare, although some portion of a resident's medical or custodial care needs may be covered by one or both. Long-term care insurance will usually (but not always) cover ALR costs, which can range from $1,500 to $6,500 a month.

Another level of care is the Enhanced Assisted Living Residence (EALR). These facilities enable persons who require significant assistance with daily needs, such as assistance walking or who may be incontinent, to reside as independently as possible. With limited exceptions, EALRs are not suitable for persons requiring 24-hour skilled nursing care.

New York also features several facilities covered under the Assisted Living Program (ALP). An ALP is available to persons medically eligible for nursing home coverage but can be cared for in a less intensive setting. Unlike ALRs, payment for residency at an ALP *may* be covered under the Medicaid program. To be eligible, the resident may retain "non-exempt" resources of up to $16,800, and in 2022 could retain monthly income of $1,535 per month. Since an ALP is under the Community Medicaid program, there are presently no asset transfer penalties or "look-back" periods imposed for Medicaid eligibility, unlike the nursing home Medicaid program that incorporates a five-year look-back period and imposes asset transfer penalties for non-exempt asset transfers made within the five-year look-back period.

While ALPs are attractive on many levels as of 2021 there were only 10,159 ALP beds throughout New York State (about one-third of New York counties have no ALP beds)[32], leaving many otherwise eligible people searching for other options.

Nursing Home Care

While most people with failing health begin receiving care in a home or assisted living setting, inevitably a significant number of

---

[32] Source: http://wnylc.com/health/entry/150/

them will see their health decline to the extent that many will require nursing home care.

The reality today is that nursing home costs are beyond the reach of most people. Nationally, the price of a semi-private nursing home room in 2021 averaged $94,900 per year.[33] But the costs in many parts of the country far exceed that figure. In the New York metropolitan area, for example, the cost for a year as a private-pay resident in a nursing home will typically exceed $175,000!

Since residing in a nursing home even just a few years as a private pay resident can wipe out a lifetime of savings for the average American, not surprisingly, people are eager to preserve as much of their assets as possible for themselves, their children, and other loved ones. All too often, however, people faced with an impending long-term care crisis will haphazardly make gifts of assets to their children, only to run afoul of the rules that impose financial "penalties" for gifts made too close to the filing of a Medicaid application.

The Look-Back & Penalty Periods

Unlike most states' Community Medicaid programs that allow for Medicaid eligibility as soon as one month after assets have been transferred out of the applicants' name, nursing home Medicaid eligibility is subject to a more stringent set of rules that restrict an applicant's ability to give away most of their assets to achieve immediate Medicaid eligibility. Under the Deficit Reduction Act of 2005, there is presently a five-year "look-back" period for nonexempt asset transfers for nursing home Medicaid. This means that when an application for nursing home Medicaid is filed, the local Medicaid agency will scrutinize the applicant's accounts and

---

[33] Source: https://www.medicaidplanningassistance.org/nursing-home-costs/

other assets to determine if, within five years from applying (e.g., the "snapshot" date), the applicant has made any non-exempt transfers for Medicaid purposes.

You may now ask, "how does the Medicaid office obtain five years' worth of the applicant's financial records?" It is the applicant's obligation to provide to the Medicaid office *every* account statement for *every* financial account in which the applicant had an ownership interest over the preceding five years—including bank accounts, investment accounts, stocks, bonds, life insurance, annuities, IRAs, 401ks, and other retirement accounts. Since it often falls upon one or more of the applicant's children to accumulate this information for a parent with dementia or who is otherwise in failing health, it is often a daunting task.

If it is determined that there have in fact been nonexempt transfers during the look-back period, these transfers will result in the Medicaid applicant being rendered ineligible for nursing home Medicaid for a period determined by calculating the amount of total non-exempt transfers made during the look-back period divided by the "Regional Rate" then in effect for the Medicaid region in which the application is filed. Regional Rates vary widely between states, and often even within a single state. North Carolina and Florida, for instance, both use a statewide Regional Rate. In 2022 North Carolina's Regional Rate was $6,810.00, while Florida's Regional Rate was $9,703.00. New York, on the other hand, divides the state into seven distinct regions for Regional Rate purposes in recognition of the widely divergent costs of care in different areas of the state. In 2022 the figures ranged from a high of $14,012 for Long Island, and a low of $11,328 for the "Central" region comprising less affluent areas in rural upstate New York.

How then is a nursing home Medicaid penalty period determined? Assume a widowed applicant named "Ralph Jones" moves into a nursing home in his home county of Orange County, New York. At the time he entered the nursing home his son Albert, as Ralph's agent-in-fact under a Power of Attorney, signed a nursing home admission agreement on Ralph's behalf. Under the admission agreement, Albert agreed to use his father's assets to pay for his father's cost of care.

Soon after Ralph entered the nursing home, however, Albert, upon the advice of his friend at work, Stanley, transferred $200,000 from Ralph's bank accounts to Albert and his sister Laura. After the asset transfers Ralph had "countable resources" below the 2022 eligibility threshold of $16,800, and Albert promptly filed a Medicaid application on Ralph's behalf. Since Ralph is in the "Northern Metropolitan" region, the 2022 monthly divisor used by the Orange County Department of Social Services (DSS) to determine the Medicaid penalty period was $13,399. DSS will divide the $200,000 in nonexempt transfers by $13,399, resulting in just under a 15-month period of Medicaid ineligibility.

This means for Ralph that Medicaid will pick-up the cost of his care, but only *after* 15 months have elapsed. The problem here is that Ralph no longer has the means to pay for the cost of his care during the 15-month period that Medicaid will not cover those expenses. Within a month or two of not being paid, the nursing home inevitably will sue Ralph and most likely his children to whom the gifts were made. If payment is not promptly made, the nursing home might also sue to "evict" Ralph from the nursing home. The situation would be especially dire if Albert and Laura no longer had the gifted funds because, as often is the case, they had already used the money to pay for their own personal expenses.

The Family Home Exemption

The old cliché that a person's "home is their castle," still rings true today. People are typically more concerned with protecting the value of their home than any other asset. The government also recognizes the importance of the home, providing for special protections if a homeowner requires long-term care.

Under current Medicaid law, and subject to one important exception, a home remains an "exempt" asset (e.g., is not treated as a countable resource) when the homeowner applies for Medicaid if the applicant, the applicant's spouse and/or a minor or disabled child reside in the home. This exemption, however, is subject to an equity "cap," which is adjusted annually and may differ from state-to-state. In 2022, the New York equity exemption is $955,000, which is the maximum amount permitted under federal law. This cap means that if, for example, a person had a home valued in 2022 at $1 million, $45,000 of the equity value is deemed nonexempt (and unprotected) for Medicaid purposes.

A Medicaid applicant who enters a long-term care facility without a "qualifying" relative remaining in the home can have the home remain exempt when filing a Medicaid application, so long as they file a "statement of intent to return home" with the application. However, while the person's Medicaid eligibility will not be generally affected, the Medicaid agency may impose a lien against the home up to the amount of Medicaid benefits paid; the lien must be satisfied at the time the home is sold, whether during the Medicaid recipient's lifetime or after their death. So, while the home is by law deemed "exempt" in such a circumstance the equity in the home can be quickly reduced by a Medicaid lien, rendering the exemption more of a theoretical benefit than a real one.

In such a circumstance a typical planning strategy will be to recommend that the home be sold as soon as possible to minimize the impact of a potential Medicaid lien. If the home is sold before the Medicaid agency files a lien, then a significant portion of the equity may be preserved utilizing the "half-a-loaf" strategy described later in this chapter.

Exempt Transfers for Nursing Home Medicaid

As discussed earlier in this chapter, under the Medicaid "lookback" rules gifts made by a nursing home resident within the five-year period preceding a Medicaid application are scrutinized by the local Medicaid office to determine the impact of those gifts on the applicant's Medicaid eligibility. Contrary to common perception, however, not all asset transfers made during the lookback period will cause the imposition of a period of Medicaid ineligibility. Rather, there exist several transfers that are "exempt" from the imposition of a Medicaid "penalty."

The most common exempt transfer is a gift of assets from one spouse to another. Such spouse-to-spouse gifts—regardless of the amounts transferred—are exempt from the imposition of any period of Medicaid ineligibility. Elder law attorneys will typically recommend the transfer of virtually all assets into the name of the "well" spouse to enable the "ill" spouse to become immediately eligible for nursing home Medicaid coverage. The only requirement in spousal cases is that the spouse residing in the nursing home cannot retain assets over the applicable resource allowance ($16,800 in 2022 for New York residents). Often the only asset that will remain in the name of the nursing home resident is the bank account into which his or her Social Security and pension checks are deposited.

Besides the exempt spousal transfers, there are several exempt transfers that apply to the family home, which can avoid a potential Medicaid lien described in the previous section. A home can be transferred *without Medicaid penalty* to any of the following:

- A spouse

- A child under the age of 21

- A blind or disabled child of any age

- A sibling who has an "equity interest" in the home (which can include payment for taxes and household expenses) and who has lived in the home for at least a year before the Medicaid application is filed

- A "caretaker" child who has lived in the parent's home for at least two years before the Medicaid application is filed

Besides transferring a home to a spouse, the most common exempt transfer of a residence is to the "caretaker" child. To qualify for the exemption, the child need not have any credentials as a health care provider. Rather, the child who has lived with a parent for at least the two-year period must establish to the Medicaid office's satisfaction that the child has provided needed assistance to the parent. Such assistance will usually include cooking; dispensing medication; shopping for the parent, and assistance with dressing, bathing, and similar daily tasks.

Another exempt transfer is the funding of a Medicaid applicant's assets into a Supplemental Needs Trust for the *sole benefit* of a disabled family member, provided that such disabled person is under the age of 65 when the transfer is made. This exemption is permitted under the law on public policy grounds. The federal government recognizes that absent the use of assets from a parent or grandparent to help support the disabled child or grandchild, the disabled person most likely rely on governmental programs to provide for their daily needs. Allowing an elderly parent's or grandparent's assets to fund a Supplemental Needs Trust for a younger disabled child or grandchild can help reduce that person's reliance on public assistance. Note that upon the disabled beneficiary's death, any assets remaining in this type of two b Trust must vest in the disabled beneficiary's estate and are therefore subject to recovery by the state to recoup the cost of public benefits paid to or for the disabled beneficiary during his or her lifetime.

Yet another exception to the Medicaid penalty rules specifically authorized under the Deficit Reduction Act is the purchase of a life estate interest in a person's home. A purchase of a life estate is an actual purchase of real estate that automatically terminates upon the death of the purchaser, with the real property interest then passing to the person owning the "remainder" interest. While technically a life estate can be sold like any other ownership interest in real estate, it is practically impossible to sell a life estate interest, as virtually no prospective purchaser is interested in buying such a "temporary" ownership interest.

Under this exception to the Medicaid penalty rules, one criterion is that the person purchasing the life estate interest must reside in the home for a *continuous period* of at least one year from the date he or she purchases the life estate. So, this strategy is not viable for someone likely to need nursing home care soon.

Prior to 2012, New York used generous life estate tables that provided significant value to life estate interests.

> **Example:** Under the old table, a 78-year-old purchasing a life estate interest in a home valued at $600,000 could pay up to $284,940 towards the purchase of the life estate interest, since the old table calculated a life estate interest for a 78-year-old at a robust 47.049 percent interest in the total value of the property (0.47049 x 600,000 = $284,940).

The utility of this strategy in New York was reduced in 2012, however, when the state adopted the IRS' Table "S" for calculating life estate interests, which will vary depending upon the interest rate then in effect.

> **Example:** In a 2.6 percent interest rate environment, the Table S life estate interest for a 78-year-old is only 20.620 percent. In 2022, the cost for a 78-year-old to purchase a life estate in the same $600,000 house would be just $123,720, with the asset transfer available under this strategy effectively capped at the $123,720 figure, vs. the almost $285,000 amount that could have been transferred under this technique prior to 2012.

There are other downsides to this strategy. There is uncertainty on what will constitute "continuous" occupancy, for example, in the context of a "snowbird." And one must consider the possible elimination of the capital gains tax exemption available upon a later sale of the child's home. At best, the child can only claim as an exemption from capital gains tax the child's remainder interest in the home (e.g., the total value of the home, less the life estate value purchased by the parent); the parent may be able to claim an exemption on the life estate portion, so long as the parent has lived in the home for at least the two years preceding the sale. In addition, some commentators believe that the entire exemption might be deemed forfeited if the parent's purchase of the life estate interest is deemed a "sale" under the provision of the tax code that limits the exemption for capital gains for a residence to one time per owner. Under this theory, the sale of the life estate to the parent would constitute the single permitted transfer that is exempt from capital gains tax; any future sale would subject the entire gain to capital gains tax.

Based on the numerous caveats associated with the purchase of a life estate, it is a strategy with more appeal in theory than in practice.

Half-a-Loaf Planning

Even when a loved one is already in or about to enter a nursing home, it is possible to preserve a significant portion of a person's assets while still qualifying for Medicaid coverage for nursing home care expenses. For married couples, it can be as straightforward as transferring the couple's combined assets to the "well spouse," with the well spouse then executing a "spousal refusal." But for single Medicaid applicants, the solution in such a "crisis" circumstance is usually to engage in a strategy elder law attorneys typically call a "half-a-loaf" plan, which usually results in the saving of approximately one-half of the client's assets. As the old saying goes, half a loaf is better than none!

A single person residing in a nursing home will only qualify for the Medicaid program once their non-exempt assets have been reduced to the resource exemption then in effect, which in 2022 ranged from $2,000 to $16,800 depending upon the state. But simply giving away the person's assets will not result in any asset savings. As shown in the Ralph Jones example earlier in this chapter, any such nonexempt asset transfers during the look-back period will cause the imposition of a penalty period.

If in Ralph Jones's case his son Albert were to sit down with competent legal counsel, in crafting an effective "crisis" Medicaid plan, the elder law attorney would calculate Ralph's amount of excess resources, his monthly Social Security and pension income, and the private pay cost for the nursing home facility. The attorney can then determine the exact amount of resources (typically one-half or more) that will provide the maximum benefit to the family.

A half-a-loaf plan incorporates the transfer of all the client's nonexempt resources, which in Ralph's case is $200,000. But the transfer here does *not* result in a gift of the entire $200,000 to Albert and Laura. Instead, while a certain portion is still considered a gift to the children, another portion is treated as a loan that is memorialized by a promissory note, which results in a shorter penalty period and a significant amount of assets preserved for the children.

To determine how much of a person's assets can be preserved in a crisis Medicaid case, several factors must be considered: (i) the amount of excess resources, which in Ralph's case amounts to $200,000; (ii) the amount of any other non-exempt transfers made during the lookback period (assume there are none in this example); (iii) the client's total income, which for Ralph totals $3,050 per month between his Social Security and pension; and (iv) the private pay rate for the nursing home, which for our example is $12,000 per month.

Armed with these figures, the elder law attorney will run a calculation to determine the maximum amount that can be gifted to Albert and Laura. With $200,000 in excess resources, we will first assume that the gift will be one-half, or $100,000, with a loan of the remaining $100,000. A $100,000 gift would cause a penalty period of 7.46 months ($100,000 ÷ $13,399). Once he is approved for Medicaid, Ralph would be budgeted $50 per month for his personal needs allowance, resulting in a monthly "shortfall" between his remaining income ($3,000) and the monthly cost of care ($12,000) in the sum of $9,000. To determine if the total loaned amount ($100,000) will cover the monthly $9,000 shortfall during the 7.46-month penalty period, we multiply the $9,000 shortfall by 7.46 months and we find we will need $67,140 of loaned funds to cover that shortfall. Since the $100,000 of loaned funds exceeds the shortfall amount of $67,400, we can conclude that a larger total gift than $100,000 can be made.

After running a few more scenarios, we find that the optimal gift amount in our example is approximately $119,500. With a $119,500 gift divided by the Regional Rate of $13,399, we end up with a penalty period of 8.9 months. We then multiply 8.9 by the $9,000 shortfall amount and see we need available funds from the loan totaling $80,100 to cover the shortfall. Subtracting the $119,500 gift from the original $200,000 of available resources leaves us with $81,500 in funds available for the loan, which is just over the amount necessary to cover the shortfall.

The example above is a basic illustration of the half-a-loaf strategy, but other factors must be considered, including reductions of the resources available for things such as legal fees, a possible pre-need funeral contract, and a set-aside for the client's personal resource allowance.

Once the loan amount is calculated, the client would then be advised to immediately transfer the funds—both the gifted and loaned amount—to one or more children or other beneficiaries. The loan <u>must</u> be memorialized by a promissory note that is irrevocable, non-assignable, cannot be canceled upon death, and must be paid out in equal installments over a period no longer than the lender's actuarial life expectancy. In the above example, the loan term would be for nine months to cover the duration of the penalty period. A reasonable rate of interest must be charged for the note; we will typically use a rate of interest roughly equivalent to the applicable federal rate, or AFR (as of this writing the short-term AFR is just 1.26 percent).

Upon completion of these transactions, the client will be "otherwise eligible" for Medicaid, as he will have retained no more than the exempt amount of $16,800. Submission of a valid application will trigger the commencement of the 8.9-month period of Medicaid ineligibility. The promissory note payments, combined with the client's other income, are used to cover the cost of the nursing home care during the 8.9-month penalty period. After the note is fully paid, the client will be eligible to receive Medicaid benefits, and the family will be free to retain the gifted assets, thereby finalizing a successful "half-a-loaf" plan.

The Medicaid GRAT

Sometimes a half-a-loaf plan is called for but using a promissory note for repayment of the loan portion of this strategy is not a viable strategy. For example, the person needing long-term care may not have close family members who wish to be personally liable for repayment of the promissory note. In such a case a *Medicaid GRAT* may be an ideal solution.

A GRAT (short for "Grantor Retained Annuity Trust") is a form of irrevocable trust. GRATs have been traditionally used in estate planning to assist wealthy people to transfer assets to others, for example, children and grandchildren, at a discounted value for gift and estate tax purposes. But after the 2006 enactment of the Deficit Reduction Act (DRA), GRATs have been used to help preserve a client's assets when faced with an immediate long-term care crisis.

With a GRAT, the grantor establishes and funds a properly designed irrevocable trust. The trustee will typically be a corporate or other professional trustee. The GRAT must meet the DRA requirements for annuities; that is, the GRAT must be irrevocable, payments to the client from the GRAT must be actuarially sound (i.e., paid out over a period not to exceed the client's life expectancy), payments must begin immediately, and the state must be named as the primary beneficiary up to the amount of Medicaid payments paid on the client's behalf.

> **GRAT Strategy Example:** Assume an 80-year-old single woman named "Daisy" has $250,000 of assets and $1,000 of income per month. Daisy is entering a nursing home that costs $10,200 per month on a private pay basis. She may consider gifting

approximately one-half of the assets (or $125,000) to her children, either outright or into an irrevocable income only trust. The Medicaid ineligibility period that would result from that gift in Orange County, New York in 2022 would be 9.3 months. However, the ineligibility period will begin to run only when Daisy is "otherwise eligible"—that is, her assets do not exceed $16,800. To "get the clock started" on the penalty period, Daisy can fund the $125,000 remaining in her name after into a GRAT that would pay fixed monthly payments (in this case, assume $9,100 per month) during the 9.3-month Medicaid ineligibility period. The client's total income of $10,100 will cover virtually all the nursing home costs for 9.3 months; after those payments are completed and the GRAT assets are depleted, Daisy should be eligible for Medicaid coverage.

Maintaining a Paper Trail to Avoid Medicaid Penalties

When the local Medicaid office reviews the required five years' worth of financial records that must be submitted upon filing a nursing home Medicaid application, unless it can be proven that the transfers were made (i) in exchange for goods or services provided, or (ii) for a purpose other than to qualify for Medicaid, then such transfers will cause the imposition of a Medicaid penalty period. With that unfortunate result, Medicaid coverage is delayed, and the applicant's family will have to shoulder what could be tens or even hundreds of thousands of dollars in long-term care costs.

A 2013 New York appellate court case, *Donvito v. Shah*[34], provides a great example of this pitfall. Between June 2007 and

---

[34] Donvito v. Shah, 108 A.D.3d 1196, 969 N.Y.S.2d 693 (2013)

August 2008, Nicholas Donvito transferred funds totaling $54,162.05 to his son Mark and other family members. The final transfer of $6,500 was made one month after Mr. Donvito suffered a stroke, and just two months before Mr. Donvito entered a nursing home.

When Mr. Donvito subsequently applied for Medicaid nursing home coverage, the Onondaga County Department of Social Services (DSS) imposed a seven-month penalty period, which was determined by dividing the total amount of the transfers made during the look-back period by the Medicaid "Regional Rate" then in effect. The effect of the Medicaid "penalty" was that Nicholas Donvito was responsible to cover his nursing home costs during that seven-month period; since he had practically no assets the nursing home would have then looked to Mark to pay his father's nursing home bill during the penalty period. Mark, on his father's behalf, appealed the DSS determination and filed for an administrative "Fair Hearing."

At the Fair Hearing, Mark raised two issues. First, he claimed that the final $6,500 transfer from his father was for reimbursement for expenses that Mark had incurred on his father's behalf, and therefore was not a gift. Second, while conceding that the approximately $48,000 in other transfers during the look-back period were gifts, Mark claimed those transfers were part of a pattern of gift-making by his father, and therefore were made by his father for a purpose other than to qualify for Medicaid, which is a statutory exception to the penalty rules. The hearing officer disagreed, and after having their claim denied at the Fair Hearing, the Donvito family sought judicial relief.

Unfortunately for the Donvito's, they could not produce any receipts or other proof that the $6,500 transfer constituted reimbursement for expenses paid on Nicholas's behalf, so the appellate court rejected that claim. On the other transfers that were conceded to be gifts, the court held that the family had failed to prove that such gifts were motivated for a purpose *other than* to qualify Mr. Donvito for Medicaid. The court stated that, "[c]ontrary to petitioner's contention, decedent did not have a consistent history of giving money to relatives; before the transfers in question, decedent's most recent gift was seven years earlier." So, the court upheld the seven-month Medicaid penalty period imposed by the DSS.

It is common for families to transfer funds from an ill parent to children, often to reimburse the family members for expenses they have covered for their parent. As in the Donvito's situation, however, all too often the family fails to retain receipts or other evidence proving that the transfer of funds from the parent constituted legitimate reimbursement for the parent's expenses. As demonstrated by the *Donvito* case, such shoddy record-keeping may prove to be an expensive oversight if nursing home Medicaid coverage is sought within five years of any such transfers.

Protecting the "Well" Spouse

In the discussion of "Ralph's" crisis Medicaid plan discussed earlier in this chapter, Ralph was widowed. Many crisis Medicaid cases, however, involve a married couple where one spouse needs care, and the other spouse is in good (or at least better) health. The "well," or "community" spouse is understandably concerned about maintaining his or her quality of life and financial well-being if the "ill" spouse needs long-term care. Under current New York law, if one spouse needs long-term care and is seeking Medicaid, the community spouse is, at a minimum, permitted to retain the marital home and in 2022 up to $137,400 of other assets ("Community Spouse Resource Allowance," or CSRA), an automobile, household furnishings and their other personal property. As of 2022 the community spouse was also permitted to retain monthly income of $3,435 (the "Minimum Monthly Maintenance Needs Allowance," or MMMNA) before being expected to make any contribution towards the ill spouse's care.[35]

For the ill spouse to qualify for Medicaid, as of 2022 he or she cannot retain assets in his or her name exceeding $16,800. Typically, the ill spouse will transfer all his/her assets to the community spouse, except for the $16,800 allowance. A key point to reiterate is *there are no transfer penalties for asset transfers between spouses!* But what if because of the transfers the community spouse now has assets (not including the marital home, which is an "exempt" asset) exceeding the CSRA? Ordinarily, the ill spouse would not qualify for Medicaid coverage until the community spouse were to "spend down" the resources over the CSRA. However, New York—along with only Florida (and arguably Connecticut pursuant to a federal court ruling)—presently permits a technique known as "spousal refusal." Under this rule, the community spouse can submit to the Department of Social Services a written refusal to contribute towards the ill spouse's care, and the ill spouse—if they are otherwise eligible—cannot be denied Medicaid even though the community spouse may retain assets over the CSRA. While a spousal refusal will permit an ill spouse to be placed on Medicaid immediately, the county Department of Social Service retains the right to bring an action for support against the community spouse in Supreme or Family Court.

For Community Spouses with resources significantly above the CSRA level--which is frequently the case after the couple's assets have been transferred solely to the name of the Community Spouse--one planning technique is for the Community Spouse to consider using a portion of their excess resources to purchase an immediate

---

[35] The CSRA and MMMNA amounts will vary depending upon the jurisdiction; a state-by-state listing is found in *Appendix A*

annuity, which effectively converts the excess resources into a stream of income. For example, assume a Community Spouse with total excess resources of $300,000 uses those funds to purchase an immediate annuity that pays her $1,500 a year per life (the actual income stream will be determined by the Community Spouse's age at the time the annuity is purchased and the prevailing interest rate). If the Community Spouse's other income was $2,000 per month, the additional annuity income will bring her recurring income to $3,500 per month. Although that sum exceeds the MMMNA amount of $3,435, DSS may request a spousal contribution of only 25 percent of the Community Spouse's income above the MMMNA level. In the above example, the spousal contribution would be only $16.25 per month (or 25 percent of the difference between the Community Spouse's monthly income of $3,500 and the $3,435 MMMNA amount). Although in using this technique the Community Spouse may forfeit the right to receive any of the ill spouse's income, the Community Spouse would also remove any threat that they can be sued for having excess resources, which may be of paramount importance.

What If the "Well" Spouse Dies First?

When a person is facing a long-term health care crisis, their family's focus naturally turns to the needs of the person requiring care. Usually, the family will be seeking Medicaid coverage to help pay for that care. The "well" spouse and children are often consumed with compiling the requisite financial and medical records necessary to attain Medicaid eligibility and may overlook the need to protect the well spouse's assets.

To qualify the "Ill Spouse" for Medicaid coverage, in 2022 he or she must have "countable resources" valued at or below $16,800 (or less, depending on the state). Where one spouse remains in the community (called the "Community Spouse"), obtaining Medicaid approval for the Ill Spouse requires that ownership of virtually all the couple's assets will need to be transferred to the Community Spouse alone. Under the Medicaid rules, there are *no* asset transfer penalties imposed when transferring the Ill Spouse's assets or jointly held assets solely into the Community Spouse's name, with the Ill Spouse being rendered Medicaid eligible in the month after the assets have been retitled in the Community Spouse's name.

While titling virtually all the couple's assets in the name of the Community Spouse is essential to enable the Ill Spouse to qualify for Medicaid, it is a mistake to ignore the Community Spouse's planning needs once the Medicaid application is approved. Most couples that have done rudimentary estate planning have "I love you" wills. "I love you" wills typically provide that upon the death of the first spouse, all the assets will pass outright to the surviving spouse. If the Ill Spouse passes away first, the "I love you" will presents no practical problem, since the Community Spouse will simply retain the assets previously transferred into his or her name. But what if the unexpected happens and the Community Spouse dies first? If the Community Spouse's "I love you" will remains in force, then the Ill Spouse will inherit all the couple's assets, and therefore forfeit his or her Medicaid eligibility.

A simple solution is for the Community Spouse to update his or her estate plan when the ill spouse applies for Medicaid coverage. One option is for the Community Spouse to sign a new will or living trust that provides that if the Community Spouse were to predecease the Ill Spouse, the assets will bypass the surviving spouse and instead pass directly to the couple's children, either outright or in trust. If the Community Spouse is not comfortable disinheriting the ill spouse, the Community Spouse's estate plan could provide that upon his or her death, some or all the Community Spouse's assets would be held in a "supplemental needs trust" for the benefit of the Ill Spouse, with the assets to pass to the children or other beneficiaries upon the Ill Spouse's death.

Supplemental needs trusts, which are statutorily authorized under New York State law, provide a structure in which assets can be held to supplement the needs of a disabled person, while permitting the disabled person to remain eligible for various governmental benefits, including Medicaid.

One caveat: whether assets are left in a supplemental needs trust for the Ill Spouse or instead are left directly to the children or other beneficiaries, if the Ill Spouse is receiving Medicaid at the time of the Community Spouse's death, then the county Department of Social Services may enforce the Ill Spouse's statutory "elective right" to receive approximately one-third of the Community Spouse's assets. If a supplemental needs trust is used, the Community Spouse's will should provide that if the elective right is exercised, then either the remainder of the Community Spouse's assets will remain in the supplemental needs trust during the Ill Spouse's life, or the remaining assets will pass to the children or other beneficiaries. Even under that scenario, approximately two-thirds of the couple's assets will be preserved for the children or other beneficiaries.

Retirement Accounts & Medicaid

With the possible exception of a primary residence, IRAs and other retirement accounts such as 401(k)'s are often the largest asset for many seniors. When seeking Medicaid coverage for nursing home costs, many families are unaware of how a Medicaid applicant's retirement accounts may affect the applicant's Medicaid eligibility.

Under present law, a person is ineligible for Medicaid if they have assets in their name over $16,800. Whether the existence of a retirement account affects a person's Medicaid eligibility will depend upon (i) the age of the applicant, and (ii) whether the applicant is married.

With IRA's and retirement plans, April 1st of the year *after* an IRA account owner turns 72 is a key date. Until that time, the account owner is under no obligation to begin taking their "minimum distributions" under the IRS' Uniform Life Table. In the relatively infrequent case where an applicant for Medicaid is under 72 years of age, his or her retirement accounts will be an "available resource." The IRA will be subject to a Medicaid spend down unless the IRA owner has already "annuitized" the IRA and begun taking "periodic payments."

> **Example:** if a 68-year-old Medicaid applicant has a $10,000 bank account and a $100,000 IRA that has not been annuitized, absent any other planning the applicant must liquidate the IRA and spend it on their care until they have no more than the $16,800 exemption amount.

If that same IRA account owner were 73 years old, the $100,000 IRA would already be in "pay" status. The county Departments of Social Services will no longer consider the IRA as a countable resource, but instead will count the annual IRA distribution as part of the Medicaid applicant's stream of income. The applicant may retain income of $50 per month; any additional income must be contributed towards the applicant's nursing home care.

While the Departments of Social Services acknowledge that an IRA in pay status is no longer a countable resource, there is no clear consensus on the amounts that must be withdrawn annually. For an IRA account owner with a spouse living in the community, the New York Fair Hearing decisions have consistently held that the Medicaid applicant cannot be *required* to withdraw more than the minimum distributions under the Uniform Life Table promulgated by the Internal Revenue Service. A married 73-year-old with a $100,000 IRA would have a minimum distribution in that year of $3,773. The remaining $96,337 would remain exempt until the next year's minimum distribution must be withdrawn. Again, the distribution will be counted as part of the Medicaid recipient's income stream.

For single Medicaid applicants, the answer is not as clear. Some New York counties, for example, take the position that the IRA must be withdrawn by reference to the Social Security Administration life expectancy tables, which require a larger annual withdrawal than under the Uniform Life Table.

Know that a Roth IRA's is not subject to the same favorable treatment as a traditional IRA in pay status. Roths are appealing from an income tax perspective, since there are no required minimum distributions for a Roth; however, the fact that a Roth is never technically in "pay" status leaves a Roth exposed as a countable resource, regardless of the client's age or marital status.

As for retirement accounts owned by a community spouse, many states include the value of a community spouse's retirement accounts as part of the community spouse's CSRA. In New York there are several contradictory regulations and administrative directives regarding this issue. However, most practitioners believe that the weight of authority provides that a community spouse's retirement accounts that are not in pay status are resources for Medicaid purposes, while distributions from retirement accounts in pay status will be treated as income for MMMNA purposes, with the retirement accounts to be excluded for purposes of determining the CSRA.

The "Hardship" Exception to the Medicaid Penalty Rules

Previously in this chapter I discussed the general rule that nonexempt transfers made during the five-year look-back period will create a penalty period for nursing home Medicaid eligibility. The Medicaid rules, however, recognize there are legitimate circumstances where assets transferred during the look-back period cannot be readily recovered. Often the children or other recipients have spent the money, and if they don't have other assets themselves, they will likely be "judgment-proof". In such cases a nursing home's only option may be to seek Medicaid coverage on their resident's behalf under the "under hardship" exception to the Medicaid penalty rules that is incorporated in the federal and various state regulations.

An example of effectively using this strategy is found in the New York case of *In the Matter of Tarrytown Hall Care Center v. McGuire*.[36] In *McGuire,* a nursing home convinced the appellate court that Medicaid coverage was improperly denied to one of its residents by the Westchester County Department of Social Services. The resident in question had lived at the nursing home for almost three full years. Because the resident had made gift transfers during the look-back period, there was a penalty period imposed (the court's published decision does not state for how long).

After the Westchester County Department of Social Services imposed the penalty period, the nursing home filed a petition with the appellate court requesting that Medicaid coverage be provided notwithstanding the gift transfers because, the nursing home argued, the "undue hardship" exception should have applied. As the court in *McGuire* stated, undue hardship is determined to occur, "where the institutionalized individual is otherwise eligible for Medicaid, is unable to obtain appropriate medical care without the provision of Medicaid and is unable to have the transferred assets returned."

The court in *McGuire* ruled that in this instance the nursing home provided ample evidence that each prong of the "undue hardship"

---

[36] 116 A.D.3d 871 (2nd Dept. 2014)

test was demonstrated by substantial evidence, and therefore ordered the Westchester Department of Social Services to approve the nursing home's Medicaid application on its resident's behalf.

Protecting "Windfalls" For Disabled Seniors

People of all ages can suffer injuries, whether due to accidents or medical malpractice, and can inherit assets. Many people who receive such a "windfall" require significant and ongoing assistance with activities of daily living, such as ambulating, dressing, bathing, and eating. The cost of care, whether in the community or in a nursing home facility, will typically exceed three hundred dollars per day in New York's Hudson Valley region. Even recipients of inheritances or large court settlements or judgments can see those funds significantly diminish in just a few short years.

Both federal and state law provides various options to help people who receive a windfall protect some or all the amount received without having to sacrifice access to public benefit programs such as Medicaid and SSI. The rules, however, differ depending upon whether the person is under or over 65.

Public benefit programs such as Medicaid and SSI are subject to rather strict resource and income tests. For example, in 2022 Medicaid is available *only* to applicants *with countable resources* of $16,800 or less; for SSI purposes, the countable resource allowance is only $2,000 for an individual. Thus, receipt of a six- or seven-figure personal injury settlement or inheritance will ordinarily result in a loss of public benefits.

Federal and state law, however, permit various planning techniques to allow for a person's assets to be removed from the category of "countable resources." For those under 65, a common approach is to create a "self-settled" (also called "first-party") supplemental needs trust (SNT) to hold the injured person's windfall proceeds. No matter how large the inheritance or settlement award, creating and funding a self-settled SNT renders the trust assets "invisible" for purposes of determining the injured person's eligibility for Medicaid and SSI. Furthermore, the individual may transfer all his or her excess assets to the trust without incurring a transfer "penalty.

The trade-off for the immediate access to the public benefit programs is that a self-settled SNT must contain a "payback" provision specifying that, upon the injured person's death, Medicaid and SSI will be repaid for cost of services provided after the establishment and funding of the SNT. Any funds remaining after the payback may be distributed to the person's beneficiaries.

But for those 65 or older, use of a self-settled SNT is not a viable option, as funding a self-settled SNT will cause the imposition of a transfer penalty for both long-term care Medicaid[37] and SSI purposes. For example, if a 70-year-old living in Orange County, New York. were to transfer $200,000 to a self-settled SNT, the penalty period for nursing home Medicaid purposes is 14.9 months; that is, assuming the person were otherwise eligible for Medicaid—meaning they have $16,800 or less in countable resources—Medicaid would not pay for their nursing home care for just over fifteen months.

For those 65 and older for whom nursing home care is not an immediate concern, use of a *pooled trust* may be a good option. Pooled trusts, which can be used by persons of any age, are statutorily sanctioned trusts operated by not-for-profit entities. The

---

[37] The "look-back" period in New York for nursing home Medicaid services is five years and as of this writing New York plans to impose a 30-month look-back for Community Medicaid long-term care services although the effective date has been delayed until at least October 2022.

injured person can sign a "joinder agreement" to participate in the pooled trust which, as the name implies, "pools" assets or income received from hundreds or even thousands of people, with each participant having an individual sub-account. Non-medical related expenses, such as shelter costs, food, clothing, property taxes, etc., can be paid out of the pooled trust sub-account without affecting the injured person's eligibility for most public benefit programs. Upon the injured person's death, assets or income remaining in the person's sub-account must either be used to repay Medicaid for the cost of services provided to the injured person or can be used by the not-for-profit to meet the needs of other disabled beneficiaries. Some pooled trusts allow funds over the "payback" requirement to be distributed to the injured persons designated beneficiaries.

A possible impediment for a disabled person in using a self-settled SNT or a Pooled Income Trust is that the person would need to give up significant control over the inherited assets, as she would be ineligible to be the Trustee of either trust and would have no say in how the assets are invested or distributed for her benefit.

But a disabled person under 65 may have another choice: she can take advantage of the Medicaid expansion under the Affordable Care Act (ACA). If the disabled person's modified adjusted gross income in 2022 is between $12,760 and $51,040 she will qualify for Medicaid health coverage and be eligible for subsidies available under the ACA. Significantly, eligibility for Medicaid under the ACA is solely determined by income, and an eligible person would not need to transfer the windfall proceeds into a "payback" trust to remain Medicaid-eligible. Instead, that person may transfer the assets into a Medicaid Asset Protection Trust (MAPT) so that should she someday apply for nursing home Medicaid coverage after expiration of the five-year "look-back" period, none of the assets held in the MAPT will be subject to a spend-down requirement before she can obtain long-term care Medicaid coverage. And unlike the first party SNT, the beneficiary can be a Trustee of the MAPT.

For a person 65 or older who requires nursing home care, transferring assets to a pooled trust within five years of admission to a nursing home will cause a Medicaid transfer penalty. In such cases, use of a "half-a-loaf" strategy described earlier in this chapter is usually the best option.

Am I legally Responsible for a Loved One's Long-term Care Costs?

When an elderly or disabled person applies for Medicaid, family members often ask, "am I responsible to contribute towards my loved one's cost of care?" Under state and federal law, an individual is legally responsible to contribute towards the care for his or her spouse and a child or stepchild under the age of 21. In cases where an individual is applying for Medicaid, the income and assets of a "legally responsible relative" will be considered by the Department of Social Services in determining the spouse or minor child's Medicaid eligibility. Also, the parents of a minor child expected to reside in a medical institution for 30 days or more will not have their assets or income considered in determining the child's Medicaid eligibility for the period that the child resides in the institution. However, if the child returns to the parents' home, the parents must assume the costs of the child's medical care.

It may be a surprise to many people that 29 states have "filial support" statutes that at least technically impose an obligation upon children to reimburse hospitals, nursing homes, and other health care providers for benefits provided to a parent. But to date there are cases in only a handful of states, including North and South Dakota, and Pennsylvania, where filial support statutes have been enforced and adult children have been held liable to pay for health care costs on behalf of a parent. A limited exception to legal responsibility is spousal or parental refusal, which is presently applied in only New York, Connecticut, and Florida. Under the "refusal" rules, an otherwise legally responsible spouse or parent can sign a statement refusing to contribute their assets and/or income towards the cost of care of a spouse or minor child. Upon receipt of a refusal notice, the Medicaid office must evaluate the "ill" spouse or child's Medicaid application *without* considering the assets or income of the spouse or parent who signed the refusal. However, even when a refusal is filed, the refusing spouse or parent must provide to the Medicaid office documentation regarding his or her assets and income. Absent such documentation, the ill spouse or child will be denied Medicaid.

While a refusal (accompanied by the necessary financial documentation) safeguards the spouse or parent's assets and income from the cost of care for an otherwise eligible spouse or child, the refusing party may still retain liability towards his or her loved one's cost of care. Under state law, a Medicaid applicant must assign to the State the right to pursue a support action against the refusing party. While years ago Medicaid offices rarely brought support actions against a refusing spouse or parent, in recent years many Medicaid agencies have taken a more aggressive approach and have brought court actions seeking contributions from refusing spouses and parents. While shrinking Medicaid budgets will likely lead to a rise in the number of support actions, the refusal strategy should remain a viable planning tool for the foreseeable future in those jurisdictions where it is available.

The Perils of "Do-it-Yourself" Medicaid Planning

Many people know that most (but not all) gifts of assets made by a person within the five-year look-back period prior to filing a nursing home Medicaid application will cause the imposition of a penalty period. For example, if a nursing home Medicaid applicant living in New York's "Northern Metropolitan" region were to make non-exempt gifts totaling $100,000 during the look-back period, then assuming the applicant is "otherwise eligible" for Medicaid coverage – meaning that his countable resources do not exceed $16,800 – Medicaid will not pick up the cost of his nursing home care for 7.5 months after the Medicaid approval.

Given that a person with just under $17,000 of resources obviously cannot afford to privately pay for nine months of nursing home costs in an amount averaging almost $13,000 *per month*, the preferred strategy is to try to return the gifted assets to reduce the penalty period. Of course, this strategy requires that the persons who received the gifted assets—usually the applicant's children—still have the funds available to return. If the assets are available to be returned *prior to* the determination of Medicaid eligibility, then the family can engage in a "half-a-loaf" strategy described earlier in this chapter.

The return of gifted assets described above, however, will undo the negative result created by the original gift of all the Medicaid applicant's excess resources *only if* the assets are returned *prior to* a determination of Medicaid eligibility. This unfortunate result was confirmed in *Aplin v. McCrossen*,[38] a 2014 case decided in a New York federal district court that held that a return of gifted assets made *after* a Medicaid determination, while reducing the penalty period, will also result in the start date for the penalty period being pushed back to a later date.

The detrimental effect of this court-approved policy can be seen by a review of the facts in *Aplin*. There, the Medicaid applicant had gifted to family members a total of $380,000 during the look-back period, resulting in a 47.48-month penalty period starting

---

[38] Aplin v. McCrossen, No. 12-CV-6312FPG, 2014 WL 4245985 (W.D.N.Y. Aug. 26, 2014)

November 1, 2007. The family then returned some of the gifted amounts, intending to provide resources for Ms. Aplin to cover the nursing home costs during the now-reduced penalty period.

While the Wayne County DSS agreed that the return of gifts resulted in a reduction of the penalty period, DSS also moved the beginning of the look-back period from November 1, 2007 to July 1, 2009. DSS argued—and the Federal Court agreed—that the returned gifts technically changed the Medicaid applicant's eligibility status as of the original Medicaid determination date, and therefore Ms. Aplin had to privately pay for the cost of her care for the period between November 2007 and July 2009, *and for the entire new penalty period* to begin as of July 1, 2009.

The practical effect of the *Aplin* court's ruling is that <u>once a Medicaid eligibility determination has been made</u>, the applicant is "stuck" with the penalty period created by the gifts made during the look-back period. Once a penalty period has been properly determined by the Department of Social Services, it is simply <u>too late</u> to attempt "corrective" Medicaid planning.

The solution is to retain elder law counsel experienced in "crisis" Medicaid planning *before* a Nursing Home Medicaid application is filed! Nursing homes will often suggest that the family allow the nursing home to file the Medicaid application on the resident's behalf. But allowing the nursing home to apply often results in losing tens or even hundreds of thousands of dollars to the family. I have seen many instances where nursing homes routinely apply even if the applicant has countable resources over the resource exemption then in effect. As a result, the Medicaid application will be denied, leaving the resident on the hook for the cost of care at the nursing home's private pay rate.

Another 2014 New York case, *Aaron Manor Rehabilitation and Nursing Center, LLC v. Diogo*[39], is likewise instructive. In 2011 Grace Diogo was admitted to a nursing home by her niece, Annette Louis. Ms. Louis, who Grace had designated as agent under Grace's power of attorney, signed the nursing home admission agreement on her aunt's behalf. Under the admission agreement, Mr. Louis agreed to use Ms. Diogo's assets to pay for Ms. Diogo's cost of care, and to apply for Medicaid for Ms. Diogo. In 2009—two years before Ms. Louis signed the nursing home admission agreement for her aunt—Ms. Diogo had given Ms. Louis and her mother $24,000 apiece. Since those transfers constituted nonexempt transfers that were made during the five-year look-back period, they resulted in a Medicaid "penalty period" of approximately five months, during which the nursing home was not paid by either Ms. Diogo—who by 2011 was essentially out of money—or Medicaid.

Evidently not pleased to be left holding the bag, the nursing home sued Ms. Diogo and Ms. Louis for over $62,000, asserting several contractual and tort claims including breach of contract, unjust enrichment, and fraudulent conveyance. Central to the nursing home's position was the signed nursing home admission agreement that required Ms. Diogo and her agent, Ms. Louis, to use Ms. Diogo's funds to cover the cost of care. Among other claims, the nursing home asserted that the 2009 transfers constituted a breach of that promise, since those transfers during the penalty period left Ms. Diogo unable to cover the cost of her care during the resulting Medicaid penalty period.

In its decision, the New York appeals court granted the nursing home's motion for summary judgment that Ms. Diogo and Ms.

---

[39] *Aaron Manor Rehab. & Nursing Ctr., LLC v. Diogo*, 114 A.D.3d 1266, 981 N.Y.S.2d 237 (2014).

Louis were in breach of contract but denied the nursing home's motion for summary judgment on the claims that the defendants were "unjustly enriched," and that their actions constituted a "fraudulent conveyance." The Court held that Ms. Diogo and Ms. Louis had raised genuine issues of fact as to whether the 2009 transfers constituted a "fraudulent conveyance," and whether Ms. Louis had acted in compliance with the nursing home agreement. The matter was returned to the trial court for further proceedings.

But even though Ms. Diogo and Ms. Louis' may have partially "won" the case at the appellate level, in a practical sense they had already lost. Ms. Louis would have almost certainly spent many thousands of dollars on legal fees, and barring a prompt settlement after the court decision, she was almost certain to spend many more thousands of dollars in fees, with no guarantee they would prevail at trial.

A 2013 Bankruptcy Court case, *In Re Woodworth*,[40] provides another example of the perils of do-it-yourself asset preservation planning. In *Woodworth*, a woman named Dorothy Stutesman transferred assets in an investment account valued at $142,742 to her daughter, Holly Woodworth. Mrs. Stutesman testified before the Bankruptcy Court that she was unsophisticated about finances, and that she transferred the assets to her daughter to both protect the assets from potential "scammers," and to enable her "to be eligible for Medicaid and other public benefits, should there come a time when she needed such benefits." Mrs. Stutesman testified that she considered the funds to be her own assets and not her daughter's, notwithstanding that they were titled in her daughter's name. Holly similarly testified that she always considered the assets as her mother's assets.

---

[40] Bankr. E.D. Va., No. 11-11-51-BFK, Feb. 6, 2013

After experiencing losses in the financial markets, in 2010—eight years after the assets were put in Woodworth's name—Mrs. Stutesman and her daughter agreed to move the funds to a new financial adviser. The new adviser convinced the women that Holly should put the assets in a trust because, among other reasons, the trust could protect the assets from Holly's creditors.

Unfortunately for Mrs. Stutesman and her daughter, Holly owned an investment property that lost value in the real estate crash and was ultimately worth less than the mortgage balance. In February 2011, Holly filed a Chapter 7 petition for bankruptcy.

During the bankruptcy proceeding, the bankruptcy Trustee correctly identified the approximately $142,000 that had been placed into the trust as a fraudulent transfer under the Federal Bankruptcy Code. However, Mrs. Stutesman and her daughter argued that the trust assets were never actually Ms. Woodworth's property, but were simply being held in trust for Mrs. Stutesman, and therefore should not have been included as part of the bankruptcy estate. In legal parlance, the women argued that Ms. Stutesman retained "equitable title" while Holly, as Trustee, held "legal title."

The Bankruptcy Court did not buy the women's argument. The Court stated that after the assets were transferred in 2002 to Holly's own investment account, she had full control to do with those assets as she wished. In citing Mrs. Stuteman's own testimony, the Court stated:

> *Ms. Stutesman can't have it both ways--she can't part with title for purposes of Medicaid eligibility, and at the same time claim that she retained an equitable title to the asset. To allow this kind of secret reservation of equitable title would be to sanction Medicaid fraud.*

Because the Court's rejected Mrs. Stuteman's and Ms. Woodworth's arguments, the entire $142,742 in the investment trust was ordered payable to the Bankruptcy Trustee to be distributed to Ms. Woodworth's creditors.

The *Woodworth* case highlights one danger when parents make outright transfers of their assets to their children, and why I almost always recommend against that strategy. However, there is a technique by which Mrs. Stutesman could have appropriately protected her assets from a potential Medicaid spend-down without exposing those assets to her daughter's creditors. Specifically, in 2002 Mrs. Stutesman could have created and funded her approximately $142,000 of assets into a "Medicaid Asset Protection Trust" (which is discussed in Chapter 15), with her daughter designated as the Trustee. Funding that trust in 2002 would have started the five-year Medicaid look-back period, which would have then run its course by 2007. Mrs. Stutesman could have retained access to the income derived from the trust assets, with the principal remaining protected. It is noteworthy there is nothing in the decision indicating that Holly gave any of the gifted assets back to her mother, which implies that Mrs. Stutesman lived comfortably on her income; this is typical of most of our clients seeking to preserve their assets from a Medicaid spend down.

Fast-forward to 2011, when Holly filed bankruptcy. Had she merely served as Trustee of her mother's trust, rather than as the owner of the gifted assets, the assets in the income-only trust would have been excluded from inclusion in Holly's bankruptcy estate, and the assets would have been preserved during her mother's lifetime. Such a trust could have been structured to provide that, upon Mrs. Stutesman's death, the assets could have remained in a trust for *Holly's* benefit, with those assets to be further protected from Holly's *current and future* creditors!

Unfortunately, it appears from reading the Court's decision that at no point did Mrs. Stutesman or her daughter seek the counsel of an elder law attorney to help them through the complex issues surrounding estate and asset preservation issues. Had they done so, the story would almost surely have resulted in a much happier ending for them; instead, the only ones left smiling were the Bankruptcy Trustee -- and Holly's creditors!

Cases such as *Aplin, Diogo,* and *Woodworth* demonstrate the risks that families undertake in trying to engage in Medicaid planning without the assistance of knowledgeable and experienced legal counsel.

VA Pensions for Long-Term Care

Many veterans of World War II, the Korean conflict, Vietnam, the Gulf War and more recent conflicts in the Middle East require assistance with the activities of daily living, either at home or in a health care facility, but have insufficient means to pay for it. Fortunately, there is a relatively little-known program known as the *Veterans Aid and Attendance* program (Aid and Attendance), that as of 2022 could provide tax-free income of up to $3,253 per month to assist eligible veterans pay for their needed care. It is estimated that up to one-third of veterans (or their surviving spouses) may be eligible for this benefit.

Veterans over the age of 65 who served during a time of war, and their surviving spouses, may be eligible for Aid and Assistance. As with most government programs, there is an income and asset test. For married couples where both spouses are qualified veterans the maximum annual benefit (known as "MAPR") in 2022 is $39,036; for a married couple where one spouse is a qualified veteran the maximum annual benefit is $29,175; while for individual veterans the maximum annual benefit in 2022 is $24,610 per year. However, individuals and couples with income much higher than the Aid and

Attendance limits may be eligible for the benefit if they have large medical expenses, which includes the costs of assisted living or similar facilities, to offset their income.

Beginning in 2018 the VA for the first time imposed a resource limit for Aid and Attendance eligibility, with the 2022 resource limit set at $138,489. While the figure does not include a personal residence, which remains an exempt resource for VA Aid and Attendance purposes, it *does* include the applicant's annual income. For example, if an applicant has countable resources of $130,000, and countable annual income of $9,000, the applicant will be deemed to have countable resources for VA pension purposes of $139,000 and is therefore ineligible for the service-connected pension.

In addition, beginning in 2018 the VA began imposing asset transfer penalties. For asset transfers to family members or to a trust made *on or after October 18, 2018*, the VA will impose transfer penalties if, within 36 months immediately preceding the date the VA receives the pension claim, an applicant transfers assets to family members or a trust over the maximum resource allowance then in effect, The calculation of the "penalty period"—which is the time that must elapse before the VA will provide a pension to an otherwise eligible applicant—will be determined by dividing the total value of the asset transfers in excess of the resource allowance by the MAPR then in effect for a veteran with a spouse or dependent child.

> **Example:** Assume that on April 20, 2022, a married disabled veteran transferred $100,000 to his son, reducing the veteran's assets to the current $138,489 resource allowance. However, the $100,000 transfer will cause a 41.14-month penalty period calculated by dividing the gift ($100,000) by the monthly MAPR for a veteran with a spouse or dependent

child ($2,331) ($100,000 ÷ $2,431 = 41.14 months). Note there is a five-year limit on the penalty period, so if instead the veteran had transferred assets totaling $200,000, then the penalty period is not 82.27 months but is capped at five years.

The penalty period begins on the first day of the month following the transfer, which in this example would be May 1, 2022. If, however, the transfer had been made on October 17, 2018, then no transfer penalty would be imposed.

More information about the Aid and Attendance program and other veterans' pension programs can be found at the United States Department of Veterans Affairs website.[41]

Crisis Medicaid Planning Case Study

When faced with an immediate health care crisis necessitating planning for a loved one's long-term care, families must know that there are options to ensure quality care without having to exhaust the entirety of the loved one's assets. Here's an example of a common situation: an adult child calls our office and tells me that her father suffered a stroke and was placed in a nursing home during the past week. The family (comprising a wife and three adult children) hopes he can return home, but that result is uncertain. Mom is relying on the children to help with the planning. She's 80 years old, but generally in good health. The couple's assets comprise a home worth $250,000, CDs totaling $300,000, and a money market account with $100,000. All the assets are owned jointly with rights of survivorship. Dad has a total income of $2,000

---

[41] Va.gov/pension/

a month, while mom's only income is her Social Security of $800 per month.

What can be done to help dad qualify for Medicaid coverage without having to spend down most of his assets? First, we would want to have all the assets, including the home, transferred to mom, leaving dad with approximately $16,000 in his name, or retained in the joint money market account, so dad's countable resources will be under the $16,800 resource exemption in effect in 2022. If dad had not previously signed a durable power of attorney authorizing mom to make such transfers, we would hope to have him sign one now. If the father does not have the requisite mental capacity to sign a power of attorney, a "single transaction" guardianship proceeding under Article 81 of the New York Mental Hygiene Law could be brought on his behalf to allow a family member to obtain the necessary legal authority.

Assuming we can make the transfers, virtually all assets can be transferred to mom's name alone. Mom may retain her income of $800 and can receive a contribution of dad's income to bring her up to the permitted monthly spousal allowance in 2022 of $3,435. Mom may retain as "exempt" assets the marital residence, and up to $137,400 of other assets. The additional assets totaling approximately $262,600 could be "spent down" to cover the husband's nursing home costs. But a few other options can be considered.

One solution available in New York is for mom to utilize a *spousal refusal*, which is a notice from the wife to the county DSS wherein mom would exercise her legal right to refuse to contribute towards her spouse's care. While spousal refusal is a perfectly legal approach, DSS retains the right to bring a support action in court against mom. To eliminate the risk of being sued, mom can consider converting most of the $262,600 of "excess" assets into an income stream, either by purchasing an immediate pay annuity, or by making a loan to the children in exchange for a non-assignable promissory note. If an annuity is selected, mom might expect to receive approximate monthly payments of $3,080 for eight years (assuming an interest rate of three percent), increasing mom's total income to approximately $6,515 per month. Under current New York policy, the Community Spouse will be requested to contribute 25 percent of her monthly income over $3,435; if mom's monthly income were now $6,515 per month, her monthly income contribution would be approximately $770 per month, with mom being allowed to retain the remainder.

If the annuity option is selected, the annuity must have certain features to avoid being deemed an available resource by DSS. Specifically, the annuity must be an "immediate pay" annuity, payable in equal payments for no greater a period than the annuitant's life expectancy, as determined under tables promulgated by the Social Security Administration. The annuity contract must also be irrevocable and non-assignable. And, if the annuity has not been fully paid prior to mom's death, the annuity must name DSS as the primary beneficiary up to the amount of any Medicaid benefits paid on the institutionalized spouse's behalf.

Remember that this example only touches upon some of the planning options available to families facing an immediate long-term care crisis. Each case must be evaluated on its own facts to determine the planning options.

PART VI: ADVANCED PLANNING STRATEGIES

Chapter 18 - Charitable Giving 101

When creating their estate plan, most people want to leave their assets to family, be it a spouse, children, and grandchildren. However, people often overlook the many rewards, both emotional and financial, of giving to charities both during lifetime and after death.

Besides the personal satisfaction inherent in charitable giving, the government provides significant incentives in the form of income, and gift and estate tax benefits to those who make charitable gifts. For some people, the tax incentives provide the sole reason a person makes a charitable gift; for others, the gift would have been made in any event, and the tax break is simply the icing on the cake.

Here are the main mechanisms for charitable giving, and some of the accompanying tax benefits:

- **Outright gifts**—the simplest form of charitable giving. A gift of cash provides a deduction on your federal income tax return and in most states with a state income tax, but only for taxpayers who itemize. The deduction is dollar-for-dollar against taxable income, up to a maximum of 50 percent of adjusted gross income, subject to adjustment for those in higher brackets. Gifts of appreciated securities allow the deduction for the fair market value of the asset, rather than its cost basis, but only up to 30 percent of adjusted gross income. This feature can provide a nice benefit for those looking to avoid capital gains taxes. Outright gifts also remove the asset and all appreciation from the donor's estate, potentially reducing estate tax liability.

- **Gifts of Life Insurance**—allows the leveraging of a gift, since the death benefit often far exceeds the premiums paid by the donor. CAVEAT: there is a loss of all income, gift, and estate tax charitable deductions if the charity lacks an "insurable interest" in the donor under state law.

- **Charitable Gift Annuities**—the donor irrevocably transfers money or property to a qualified organization in return for its promise to pay the donor, another person, or both, fixed and guaranteed payments for life. In substance, the transfer is part charitable gift and part purchase of an annuity. The older the annuitant, the larger the annual payments. The charitable contribution is the difference between the amount of money (or fair market value of securities or other property transferred) and the value of the annuity. A percentage of each annuity payment, as determined by government tables, is income tax free.

- **Split-Interest Gift Trust**—an agreement where one party receives income for a term, and another party receives the remainder. These vehicles provide significant income tax, gift tax, and estate tax benefits.

- **Charitable Remainder Trust (CRT)** – The donor transfers assets to a trust. The income beneficiary (and often a spouse or children) receives a stream of income for a term of years, or for life. Upon the death of the last remaining income beneficiary, the assets remaining in the trust pass to a qualified charitable remainder beneficiary. These trusts work well when the donor contributes appreciated assets to the trust; since a CRT is a "tax free" trust, the trustee can sell the appreciated assets without incurring a capital gains tax upon sale; the full value of the assets is then available for investment and production of income. Income payable to the donor will be taxable; HOWEVER, the donor will also receive a significant income tax deduction which, if it cannot be fully utilized in the year of the gift, can be carried over for up to five additional years. Since the remainder interest passes to a charity and not to family members, the "lost" assets can be replaced through use of a "wealth replacement trust" – simply, a life insurance trust which will pass the death benefit estate tax and income tax free to the children or other beneficiaries.

- **Charitable Lead Trust (CLT)**—essentially the opposite of the CRT; with a CLT, the *charity* receives the income for a term of years, with the remainder then passing to the donor's family, usually children or grandchildren. A CLT can be an excellent vehicle for "zeroing out" estate taxes; that is, the donor's will or revocable trust can include a CLT that is funded after the donor's death *only if* there would be an estate tax payable at that time. The will or revocable trust would include a formula to fund the CLT with those assets necessary to reduce the donor's taxable estate to zero. If there is no estate tax due at the donor's death, the CLT would not be formed unless, of course, the donor wished to make the charitable gift regardless of the estate tax issues.

A CLT may also provide the donor with significant income tax, gift tax and estate tax benefits.

Note that since Congress's 2018 enactment of the Tax Cut and Jobs Act (TCJA), income tax planning for charitable giving has become more challenging.

Before the TCJA, taxpayers could deduct virtually every charitable gift regardless of the amount and would receive a tax benefit for that deduction. But under TCJA the standard deductions have been increased, so that for many taxpayers their charitable contributions will no longer provide them a tax benefit.

In 2022 the standard deductions are $12,950 for a single filer, $19,400 for a head of household, and $25,900 for a married couple filing jointly. In 2017--before TCJA was enacted--the deductions were far lower, with the single filer deduction at only $6,350, the head of household deduction at $9,350, and the deduction for a married couple filing jointly at $12,700.

Consider the case of a married couple, John and Margaret Dough. In 2017 the Doughs donated $5,000 to charities. That year their other itemized deductions, including state and local taxes (SALT) and property taxes, totaled $25,000. With a standard deduction in 2017 of $12,700, the Doughs' itemized deductions of $30,000 far exceeded the standard deduction, and the Doughs were able to claim a charitable deduction for the entire $5,000 in charitable gifts in 2017.

In 2021 the Doughs again made total charitable contributions totaling $5,000. Their other itemized deductions totaled $9,000 and their SALT and property taxes totaled $16,000, for a total of $30,000. However, after TCJA their deduction for SALT and property taxes and state and local taxes were capped at $10,000, resulting in total permitted deductions, including the charitable deduction, of 15,000. Because their standard deduction for 2022 as a married couple filing jointly was $25,900 and their total permitted itemized deductions and charitable contributions was below that amount, the Doughs gained no additional tax benefit for the $5,000 in charitable donations, which were "swallowed up" by their $25,900 standard deduction.

But let's look at a different scenario. Assume instead of making $5,000 charitable gifts year after year, the Doughs instead elected to "bunch" their charitable contributions so that in 2022 they made $25,000 in total charitable gifts, but none for the next four years. The average amount of charitable gifts for each year remains $5,000, but now they will get the biggest tax bang for the buck. Based on the $25,000 charitable contributions in 2022, the Doughs' total itemized deductions that year would be $44,000, and they can save up to 47 percent of the $44,000 deductible amounts in income taxes. Over the succeeding four years the Doughs would still receive their $25,900 standard deduction (which likely will increase annually), even though their actual deductible payments are only $19,000 (assuming the same $9,000 in itemized deductions plus the $10,000 property and SALT tax cap).

Utilizing this strategy requires the ability to make larger charitable contributions in a single year. But for taxpayers with the financial wherewithal to bunch their charitable giving, it can be a winning approach.

Because charitable planning strategies can be complex, if you're interested in exploring such planning opportunities, retaining a knowledgeable and experienced professional team including an estate planning attorney, accountant and financial professional is a must.

Chapter 19 - QTIP Trusts

In a married couple's "typical" estate plan, upon the first spouse's death, assets are left directly to the surviving spouse. While this planning strategy is appealing in its simplicity, such planning may cause unnecessary estate taxes to be incurred, or assets may pass to unintended beneficiaries. One planning tool that can solve these problems is the *qualified terminable interest property*, or "QTIP" trust. A QTIP trust allows for assets to be left for a surviving spouse in a manner that qualifies for the estate tax marital deduction—that is, the assets in the QTIP trust are *not* included in the taxable estate of the first spouse to die – while providing the surviving spouse with full income and limited principal rights to the trust property.

Since property passing as an outright distribution to a surviving spouse will also qualify for the estate tax marital deduction, why might a person consider using a QTIP trust? Probably the most frequent use is in a second (or subsequent) marriage, where each spouse may wish to make sure that *their* assets ultimately pass to their own children, but at the same time providing economic benefit to whichever spouse is the survivor. Even in a first marriage situation, however, QTIP trusts may be attractive to help protect the assets for the children and future generations if the surviving spouse were to remarry. The QTIP trust can be structured so the surviving spouse will receive trust income and possibly some access to principal. The QTIP trust can specify that if a remarriage of the surviving spouse occurs, their new spouse would have no inheritance rights or ability to access the QTIP trust assets in the event that the surviving spouse and the new spouse were to divorce.

Most QTIP trusts are included in a will or revocable living trust and become effective after the death of the first spouse. As an alternative or supplement to these "testamentary" QTIP trusts, it is sometimes desirable to establish a "lifetime" QTIP trust. This planning technique is most often used as an estate tax planning vehicle in very large estates where one spouse owns a larger share of the couple's assets and is unwilling or unable to transfer assets directly to the surviving spouse. Even though portability (explained in Chapter 10) allows for the post-death allocation of the remainder of the first deceased spouse's estate tax exemption to the estate of the surviving spouse, that allocation is only available if the surviving spouse does *not* remarry, since the portability of a spouse's estate tax exemption is limited to use of the "last deceased" spouse's exemption. Since remarriage is such a common occurrence after the death of one spouse, portability should not be relied upon as a solution to the scenario where spouses have an imbalance of their assets.

> **Example**: assume a married couple living in New York has combined assets totaling $10 million, but the husband holds title to $9 million, with the wife having only ownership of $1 million. Were the husband to create a lifetime QTIP and fund that trust with $4 million of his assets, the QTIP can provide the wife with all trust income during her lifetime and might be structured to allow for distributions of principal, typically for the broad purposes of health, education, support, and maintenance. The wife may be a Co-trustee of the QTIP trust, or the husband may elect to name an independent trustee to serve alone. If the wife died first, her total taxable estate would be $5 million, all of which could be applied toward her New York estate tax exemption ($6,110,000 in 2022) and federal estate tax exemption, (12,060,000 in 2022). While the wife could still leave her $1 million share of the assets not held in the QTIP trust to her own children, the QTIP trust terms would presumably direct that the QTIP

assets that remain after the wife's death would be distributed to the husband's children, either outright or in trusts created for their benefit. If the husband subsequently died in 2022 with $5 million of total assets, *no* federal estate tax would be due, as the husband's personal representative could take full advantage of the $6,110,000 New York State and $12,060,00 federal estate tax deduction then in effect.

Chapter 20 - Qualified Personal Residence Trusts

One overriding theme discussed throughout this book is that most estate planning is not predicated on saving estate taxes. With a 2022 federal estate tax exemption of $12,060,000 per individual and a New York State estate tax exemption of $6,110,000, for most people estate planning is focused on personal planning issues such as asset protection for long-term care, remarriage protection, divorce protection for the children, and creditor protection. But for those families with significant wealth, reduction of estate taxes remains a planning challenge. With the value of real estate having skyrocketed in most of the United States during the COVID-19 pandemic, a *Qualified Personal Residence Trust* (QPRT) is one powerful planning tool for reducing estate and gift tax liability for a primary residence and/or a vacation home.

The QPRT is a form of irrevocable trust sanctioned by the Internal Revenue Code. QPRTs may be funded only with a personal residence and up to one vacation home. With a QPRT the homeowner (either an individual or married couple) transfers to the trust their interest in the personal residence, retaining the right to reside in the residence for a fixed number of years. During the QPRT term the donor will continue to pay property taxes and maintenance expenses for the premises and will continue to receive the benefit of real estate tax deductions. So long as the donor(s) survives the stated term of years, at the end of the term the donor's interest in the trust terminates and the residence will not be included in the donor's taxable estate for estate tax purposes. The QPRT will typically provide that ownership of the residence is transferred to the donor's children, or one or more trusts to benefit the donor's children. The donor and remainder beneficiaries will often agree that the donor will continue to reside in the residence, with the donor to pay a fair market value rental once the QPRT term has elapsed.

Transferring the residence to the QPRT constitutes a gift, but a significantly tax-favored one. Because the gift is a "deferred" gift–that is, the gift is not completed until the end of the QPRT term–the value of the gift is far below the fair market value of the property when the property is transferred to the QPRT. This result is based on the "time value of money": the longer you must wait to receive a gift, the less it is worth to the recipient. In addition, *all* the appreciation in the property value between the date of funding the QPRT and the end of the QPRT term is transferred to the beneficiaries *without* being added to the value of the gift.

> **Example**: assume that a 65-year-old woman, Betty, transfers a home worth $2 million to a QPRT with a 10-year term. If the home appreciates at four percent annually, the value at the end of 10 years would be 2,960,489. Because her children must "wait" 10 years for the gift, the value of the gift for gift tax purposes is only $1,339,880. So long as Betty survives the 10-year term, she will have effectively transferred a home with a fair market value of $2,960,489 at a gift tax value of only $1,339,880. Had she used none of her $12,060,000 gift tax exemption before creating the QPRT, she will still have $10,720,120 of her combined federal estate gift tax exemption remaining after the QPRT term expires. And because New York does not have a separate gift tax, using the QPRT will not use up any of Betty's $6,110,000 New York estate tax exemption.

What if Betty does not survive the 10-year term? Then the gift is null and void, and the full value of the property is included in her taxable estate. However, there is no other "penalty" for failing to outlive the term. While we can never know how long someone will live, choosing a realistic term based on the client's age and health is critical. The longer the term, the lower the amount of the gift and the more "leverage" that is created by the planning.

One potential downside of a QPRT is that when a residence is conveyed to a QPRT the trust assumes the existing cost basis in the property for capital gains tax purposes. As the home appreciates in value, the heirs may incur a large capital gain tax if the residence is later sold from the QPRT or by the heirs. If, however, the home remained in the original owner's taxable estate, the residence would receive a step-up in cost basis to the fair market value at the owner's death. So, in evaluating the benefits of the QPRT for a home that has seen significant appreciation, the potential estate tax savings must be weighed against the potential loss of the step-up in cost basis.

Chapter 21 - Domestic & Offshore Asset Protection Trusts

In Chapter 13 I described how a person can establish protective trusts for a spouse, children or other loved ones that will afford them access to the trust assets for their needs and wants, but at the same time shield those assets from their creditors. That leads to the logical question, "can I use trusts to protect my assets from my own creditors?"

The quick answer is yes, but there are certain caveats. As a fundamental principle, you cannot shield your assets from any existing creditors, whether or not a lawsuit has been commenced or a judgment has been entered. If, however, you have no existing creditors and have no reason to believe a lawsuit will be filed against you, there are several planning tools available that can help protect your assets from unanticipated future creditors.

It is a common misconception that a standard *revocable* trust offers asset protection. Revocable trusts are important and useful planning tools, but they provide *no* asset protection. With a revocable trust, the trustmaker retains full access to the assets, so the trustmaker's creditors retain the same right to access. However, an *irrevocable* income only trust, commonly used for Medicaid planning, may allow the trustmaker to shield the principal from any future creditors, since the trustmaker has made an irrevocable gift of the principal assets funded into the trust.

Many people would prefer to have greater access to all their assets, both income and principal, while enhancing their creditor protection. Under the laws of New York and most other states, it is impossible to create a creditor protected irrevocable trust that would permit the trustmaker to be a beneficiary of both trust income and principal. But as of 2022 there were 17 states, most prominently Alaska, Delaware, Nevada, Wyoming, and South Dakota, which have passed legislation allowing a person—including an individual residing in another state—to establish domestic asset protection trusts (DAPT). DAPTs are irrevocable trusts in which the trustmaker can remain a beneficiary and yet be protected against creditor claims. These trusts may have the additional bonus of allowing the assets funded into the trust to be considered lifetime gifts, with the appreciation of the assets excluded from the trustmaker's taxable estate. A potential disadvantage of DAPTs is there have been no reported cases testing whether a judgment obtained in one state (e.g., New York) can be enforced against a DAPT created in another state (e.g., Delaware) under the "Full Faith and Credit" clause of the U.S. Constitution.

While no asset protection strategy can be deemed "bulletproof," the offshore asset protection trust (OAPT) provides the greatest protection of assets against the claims of future creditors. OAPTs are similar in structure to DAPT's, but because they are created in foreign jurisdictions not subject to the Full Faith and Credit clause of the U.S. Constitution (e.g., Nevis, the Cook Islands, or the Bahamas), they are widely considered to provide a higher level of asset protection than an OAPT. In addition, foreign nations typically impose more stringent burdens of proof, shorter statutes of limitation and other legal hurdles that discourage a judgment creditor from pursuing their claim, and will often lead to a settlement more favorable to the judgment debtor. Disadvantages of OAPTs include the higher cost to create and maintain them, and some people may be uncomfortable dealing with the uncertainty of engaging in planning under the law of a foreign jurisdiction.

Asset protection is a legitimate, valuable part of the planning process. Remember, however, that the time to protect your assets is *before* an actual or likely creditor claim has arisen. At that point, engaging in any of the above-described asset protection strategies might be deemed invalid under the doctrine of "fraudulent conveyance," and might subject both you and your professional advisors to civil, and possibly even criminal, sanctions.

Chapter 22 - Sales to Intentionally Defective Grantor Trusts

One of the most popular strategies for high-net worth persons is the sale of assets to an *intentionally defective grantor trust* (IDGT). Why, you might ask, would someone want a trust that is "defective?" An IDGT is not in truly "defective" in the literal sense, but rather it's called a "defective" trust simply because the grantor remains obligated to pay the income tax on the income earned by the trust assets even though the grantor has no rights to receive the income or principal earned by the trust. While it may seem counterintuitive for someone to benefit by being taxed on income they never receive, for high-net worth clients, IDGTs are one of the most powerful planning tools available for efficient wealth transfers to children or other beneficiaries.

The mechanics of an IDGT are straightforward. An irrevocable trust is created for the benefit of the grantor's heirs. The trust is structured to be a grantor trust for income tax purposes by retaining one or more powers under Internal Revenue Code §§ 673 through 677. However, care must be taken when selecting which powers to use, because most powers under these sections would also cause the trust assets to be included in the grantor's estate at death under Internal Revenue Code § 2036(a) and/or § 2038. Many practitioners believe the safest power to use is a § 675(4) power to substitute assets of equal value. In 2005 and 2008 Private Letter Rulings, the IRS ruled that retention of this power did not cause estate inclusion.

After the IDGT is signed, the grantor sells assets to the IDGT expected to produce a high total return in exchange for an installment note paying the lowest interest rate permitted by law. This minimum interest rate is determined by using the federal rate (AFR), which is based on federal interest rates offered each month relative to the corresponding note term. The benefit of maximizing the gap between the return on the transferred assets and the interest rate paid by the trust on the installment note is that this excess represents a gift tax-free transfer from the grantor to the heirs. A critical component of the sale to an IDGT is that, while the value of the installment note payable to the grantor is "frozen," it is typical that the assets sold by the taxpayer to the IDGT in exchange for the note will appreciate, often significantly. The transfer tax advantages are multiplied as the value leaving the estate (e.g., the assets sold to the IDGT) will exceed the value coming back into the estate (e.g., the amount of periodic interest payments due under the note).

In the past there was a concern that the IRS might try to challenge the tax benefits by treating the income tax payments as taxable gifts from the grantor to the IDGT. The IRS looked at the issue and eventually rejected this line of thought.

And an IDGT provides other important income tax benefits. The grantor (or seller) and the trust (the IDGT) are treated as the same taxpayer. Therefore, no capital gain is recognized on the sale of assets to the IDGT. Further, interest payments received from the trust by the grantor on the note are not treated as income to the grantor because the grantor is, in effect, merely making payments to herself.

> **Example:** Sam and Sally sell $1 million of non-voting LLC units to an IDGT in exchange for an installment note. Their children are beneficiaries of the IDGT. The LLC generates taxable income of $125,000 each year. Because the trust is considered "defective" for income tax purposes, Sam and Sally will report this income on their Form 1040 income tax return and pay the income tax due. Assuming a 35 percent tax rate, the couple can effectively shift an additional $43,750 to the trust each year for the benefit of their children ($125,000 x 35 percent),

while the $125,000 continues to grow in the IDGT and outside of Sam and Sally's estate.

The entire transaction should be established and carried out with all the legal formalities of an arms-length transaction. To bolster the argument that the note qualifies as a *bona fide* debt, the transaction must be structured so the trust's debt/equity ratio is reasonable. Many commentators believe that a 10 percent gift, or a ratio of 9/1, provides a safe harbor. Typically, an IDGT will be funded with a gift approximately equal to 10 percent of the value of the assets to be sold to the IDGT. This gift component is the *"seed gift."*

Getting enough seed money into a trust is not always easy. If the sale is large or the seller has used up most of her applicable exclusion amount, the seller could have a gift tax to pay when the trust is seeded. Some practitioners believe this problem can be solved by using beneficiary guarantees as a substitute for seed gift. In a 1995 Private Letter Ruling, the IRS held that such a guarantee would suffice in the context of a private annuity sale, provided that the guarantor had sufficient personal assets to make good on the guarantee. So, guarantees can work, provided everything is properly documented.

PART VII: ESTATE SETTLEMENT & BEYOND

Chapter 23 - Settling an Estate

People typically have only a vague idea of the steps necessary to settle an estate upon a person's death. They have often heard "horror stories" regarding the expense and time to complete an estate administration. While there are instances where estate settlements have dragged on for years and have cost the estate hundreds of thousands of dollars in legal fees and other administration expenses, it need not be that way.

Estate settlement is largely dictated by the form of ownership of the assets possessed by the decedent. Assets owned in the decedent's individual name are typically subject to the probate process, whether or not the decedent has executed a will. But for many people, a significant portion of their assets are not owned in their individual name. Rather, assets may be owned jointly with another person, or the assets may pass to one or more persons who are the named beneficiaries designated to receive the assets at the decedent's death (for example, a bank account that includes an "in trust for" designation). All such assets will not pass as dictated in the decedent's will, but instead will pass to the surviving joint owner or the designated beneficiary outside of probate.

Assets held in a revocable or irrevocable living trust will be distributed as provided in the trust document and will not be subject to the probate process. This result can be especially helpful when a person owns real estate in more than one state, or desires to disinherit children or other close relatives. If the trust is fully funded by the client during his or her lifetime, the probate process can be avoided and there will be no legal requirement to notify potentially litigious children or other relatives about the decedent's assets and dispositive wishes.

Whether a will or a trust has been used as the foundational estate planning tool, all estate administrations must follow certain procedural steps. These steps include income tax return filings, and possibly the need to file federal and state estate tax returns. Since a probate estate is a taxpaying entity, the executor of a probate estate will obtain a federal taxpayer identification number for the estate. Trustees of any trusts created by the decedent's will also need to obtain taxpayer identification numbers for those trusts. Whether the estate and/or trust(s) will owe federal or state income taxes depends upon the types of assets owned by the various entities, and the income produced.

Estates having assets over the estate tax exemption in effect in the year of death will require filing a federal estate tax return and may also require filing a state estate tax and/or an inheritance tax return depending upon the decedent's state of residence. Whether any estate taxes are ultimately due depends upon many complex factors, especially: whether the decedent is survived by a spouse; where the decedent resided and owned property; and how the assets are to be distributed upon the decedent's death. Even where no estate taxes are owed, the returns must be filed if the minimum asset threshold is reached.

One caveat: people have often been led to believe that if you have a living trust, the estate settlement requirements will not apply to your estate. While a fully funded living trust will "avoid probate," all other estate administration requirements described above will apply. While living trusts can be exceptional planning tools, establishing one to avoid post-death administration (and all associated expenses) is unrealistic. Ignoring the formalities of the estate administration process based on such misinformation can lead to trouble later, which may include the IRS or your state assessing interest and penalties for failing to timely file the requisite tax returns and pay the required taxes.

An Estate Plan Gone Awry

While a properly designed, fully funded estate plan should be straightforward to administer, there are countless examples where poor planning has led to disastrous results. A 2017 New York case, *In the Mater of the Account of the Proceedings of DS, as Executor of the Estate of Barbara Ann Schwartz*[42], provides a stark reminder that without proper planning and implementation estate planning can lead to unintended results.

The basic facts as described in the opinion: Barbara Ann Schwartz executed her Will on April 30, 2006, which was drafted by her "friend and attorney [DS]." Curiously the attorney's full name is not revealed, but instead the judge used only the attorney's initials throughout the written opinion. The beneficiaries were Mrs. Schwartz's stepdaughter, her step grandson, and a close friend. On May 8, 2006, Mrs. Schwartz died, a mere week after she signed the will.

The estate assets were worth approximately $2.1 million, with most of that value, or about $1.6 million, attributable to Mrs. Schwartz's New York City Co-operative apartment. "DS," who of course drafted the will, was named executor, and received preliminary appointment as Executor by the New York County Surrogate in July 2006. A "full" appointment wasn't made until February 2008.

Based on the value of the assets in the estate as of Mrs. Schwartz's date of death, attorney DS would have had to file an estate tax return, and some amount of federal and New York estate tax would likely have been due. But in other respects, the estate should have been simple to administer, as the co-op comprised

---

[42] 2017 NY Slip Op 32138(U) (Sur. Ct., NY Cty., Oct. 12, 2017)

about 75 percent of the total estate value. As the facts show, however, nothing about this administration seemed routine.

For several years DS apparently did little to advance the estate administration. In April 2014, *eight years* after Mrs. Schwartz's death, Schwartz's stepdaughter hired an attorney to file a petition to compel DS to account for his actions as Executor and attorney for the estate. In his filed accounting, DS stunningly claimed he performed 1,700 hours of work and was owed a legal fee of *$499,622.50*, plus disbursements of over $2,000. Adding insult to injury, DS allegedly paid an *additional* $83,158.89 to other professionals who supposedly provided additional legal and accounting services to the estate. The total fee request amounted to a whopping *28 percent of the value of the estate*!

In Judge Rita Mella's analysis, she pointed out numerous examples of inefficiencies in DS's time records. In one of many examples, DS claimed to have spent 38 hours drafting an amended probate petition, which, the judge noted, is "a fairly straightforward document." Based on my experience, I would be hard-pressed to imagine a scenario where an amended probate petition would take more than a couple hours to complete.

In summarizing her conclusions, Judge Mella noted that DS's fee request "without a doubt" was "far in excess of a typical fee for an estate of this size and complexity," and that DS's requested fee for an estate, "which, after more than 10 years is not yet fully administered and did not present particularly complex issue, represents too large a percentage of the value of the estate's assets and is not warranted." But despite her scathing analysis of DS's reckless billing practices and incompetent handling of the estate, the Judge nonetheless approved a legal fee to DS of $175,000.

The *Schwartz* case highlights the importance of seeking competent and experienced counsel to handle estate matters. Mrs.

Schwartz made the error of hiring her "friend" to prepare Mrs. Schwartz's will, and DS likely convinced Mrs. Schwartz to name DS as the Executor. Sadly for her beneficiaries, DS proved anything but Mrs. Schwartz's friend, and his incompetence and grossly excessive legal fee request is a stain on the legal profession. While Judge Mella did authorize a fee significantly less than the outlandish amount DS requested, based on the egregious fact not only should DS have been denied a legal fee, but he seems fortunate not to have been formally sanctioned by the court for his mismanagement of the estate.

Powers of Appointment

A problem common to many estate plans is that they lack enough flexibility and control. Too often the "wrong" beneficiaries ultimately receive the assets, or even if they are the "right" beneficiaries, they receive their inheritance in a way that leaves the assets exposed to the beneficiary's creditors, a divorcing spouse, and leaves him or her unprotected from a Medicaid spend down should the beneficiary suffer an illness or injury and seek public benefits.

Fortunately, there is a planning tool available that provides enormous flexibility to deal with changing circumstances: the *power of appointment*. A power of appointment is a legal device that allows for the creator of a will or a trust to grant to another person -- or even retain for themselves -- the power to change the beneficiaries named in the instrument, or the manner in which the beneficiaries receive their inheritance.

> **Example:** Tom and Mary Jones are a married couple in their fifties. They have two children, John and Linda, who are both in their early twenties. Tom and Mary execute wills providing that, upon the first spouse's death, the deceased spouse's assets are left

in a protective marital trust for the surviving spouse. After the second spouse's death, the assets pass outright to John and Linda, in equal shares.

Tom dies suddenly at age 60 with assets of $750,000 in his name. After Tom's will is probated, those assets then are held in the marital trust for Mary's benefit. But because Tom's will did not provide Mary with a power to appoint the assets in the marital trust, she is "stuck" with the provision that the marital trust assets be distributed equally to the children upon her death, regardless of any change in circumstances.

Here's an example where such a limitation can prove problematic: assume that John, who foolishly purchases only the state minimum vehicle liability insurance of $50,000, were to cause an automobile accident that results in the deaths of two people in the other vehicle. After trial, a multi-million-dollar verdict is rendered against him. In such a case, were John to inherit the assets from the marital trust "outright" as provided under Tom's will, John's creditors would be legally entitled to seize John's inheritance in its entirety.

But what if Tom's will had instead included a provision granting to Mary a limited power of appointment authorizing Mary to alter the disposition of the marital trust assets? In such a case Mary, by executing a new will or trust, could specify that upon her death, the assets passing to the children from both Mary's own estate and under the marital trust created under Tom's will would pass into *lifetime protective trusts* for both John and Linda. Upon Mary's death, John's share of his parents' inheritance would then be protected from the reach of his creditors and instead could be used for John's benefit throughout his lifetime.

Powers of appointment can also be used to preserve "bloodline protection."

> **Example:** Were Tom and Mary to create lifetime protective trusts in their wills for the benefit of John and Linda, they could include provisions granting to their children a power to appoint, via the child's own will or trust, the assets remaining in the children's lifetime trusts to any of the child's descendants, or perhaps any of Tom and Mary's descendants. If desired, the power of appointment can be expanded to include other persons or entities, such as a child's spouse or charities, as permissible appointees.

A person can even reserve to themselves the ability to exercise a power of appointment. Such powers are regularly included in Medicaid Asset Protection Trusts (MAPT), which are irrevocable trusts. By reserving to the trustmaker the power to change the trust beneficiaries under a subsequently executed will or another trust instrument, the trustmaker retains significant control over the ultimate disposition of the trust assets upon their death. If, for instance, a parent was to have a falling out with a child after creation of the MAPT, the parent could simply execute a new will that exercises the retained power of appointment to disinherit the "wayward" child. But even if the retained power of appointment in the MAPT is never activated, its mere inclusion in the trust provides a significant benefit, as it ensures that the trust assets are deemed includable in the trustmaker's taxable estate at death, causing all the assets in the Trust to receive a stepped-up cost basis as of the date of the trustmaker's death. Estate inclusion may provide heirs with capital gains tax savings of tens or even hundreds of thousands of dollars if the children were to sell the inherited assets after the parents' deaths. MAPTs are discussed in more detail in Chapter 15.

Disclaimers: An After-Death Planning Tool

One hallmark of an effective estate plan is "controlled flexibility"—that is, a plan that accomplishes the client's objectives, but within a flexible framework that allows for adjustments necessitated by a changing landscape. A "disclaimer" is a planning tool that provides *after death* planning flexibility. Disclaimers are most effective when the strategy is considered—and planned for—during the client's lifetime.

A disclaimer in an irrevocable and unqualified refusal to accept an interest in property. The effect of a disclaimer is as if no transfer of property was made to the person making the disclaimer. Under federal law[43], the general rules for a valid disclaimer include (i) the person making a disclaimer must do so no more than nine months after the date of transfer (usually the date of death of the person from whom the property is being disclaimed), (ii) the person making the disclaimer can have accepted no part of the property interest, or any benefits therefrom, and (iii) the disclaimed property must pass with no direction by the person making the disclaimer. The laws of most states, including New York, track the federal rules.

Why would anyone willingly forego an interest in property? There are any number of both tax and non-tax reasons.

> **Example**: assume a New York resident named "Joe" died in 2020 with an estate worth $11 million. Assume further that Joe's will provided that his entire probate estate was to pass to his wife "Sarah." Sarah also has assets in her name worth $11 million. If Sarah keeps all of Joe's assets and then were to die

---

[43] 26 U.S. Code § 2518

in 2022, Sarah's personal representative could utilize portability (discussed in Chapter 10) to avoid imposition of federal estate tax on the combined $22 million estate. However, because New York law does not recognize portability, Sarah's personal representative could only utilize Sarah's individual New York estate tax exemption ($6,110,000 in 2022), resulting in the imposition of a New York estate tax of a whopping $2,986,800.

If, however, Joe's will provided that any property disclaimed by Sarah were to pass into a "credit shelter trust" created under the Joe's will for the benefit of Sarah and their children, Sarah might disclaim $6,110,00 from Joe's estate, which would then pass into the credit shelter trust. Upon Sarah's death in 2022, $15,890,000 of total assets would be subject to New York estate taxes, which equates to a total New York state tax of $2,009,200 – or $977,600 *less* than would be incurred without the disclaimer.

Critical to the success of the disclaimer in the above example is that Joe's will already included the specific language that provided for the disposition of the assets to the credit shelter trust if Sarah were to disclaim. Absent such provisions, upon Sarah's disclaimer the disclaimed assets would pass directly to the children. Usually, a surviving spouse does not want the assets to pass directly to children during her lifetime but might be more willing to disclaim if she can benefit from the assets left in the trust.

Example: "Fred's" will left one-half of his assets to his second wife, "Joan," and one-half of the assets to his four children from his first marriage. Fred was revising his estate plan when he died suddenly in

2021. However, the dispositions in Fred's will were rendered largely moot, as the majority of his $2 million in assets were in bank accounts left "in trust for" Joan. Here Joan graciously helped effectuate Fred's wishes by disclaiming several bank accounts. Because of the disclaimer, those assets passed as if Joan predeceased Fred, and under Fred's will those assets passed to his children.

Could Joan have simply taken the accounts and gifted the assets to Fred's children? While she could have taken that route, any gifts over $16,000 per year per beneficiary would have affected Joan's own estate and gift tax exemptions. Utilizing a disclaimer avoided use of those valuable tax exemptions.

Promoting Values: Ethical Wills & Incentive Trusts

A landmark 2012 study conducted by the Allianz Life Insurance Company found that 86 percent of baby boomers and 74 percent of "elders" age 72 and older believe that the non-financial values the parents will leave behind—such as ethics, morals, life lessons, faith and religion—are more important to both the children and the parents than the financial resources passed down to the next generation.[44] And yet when we discuss what typically comprises an "estate plan," rarely are the non-financial aspects addressed. Instead, the planning documents typically comprise sterile legal jargon that only addresses passing monetary assets to the future generations, with no discussion of the non-monetary legacy.

---

[44] https://www.allianzlife.com/~/media/files/allianz/documents/ent_1371_n.pdf?la=en

That's where the *ethical will* comes in. An ethical will is not a legal document. Rather, it can be thought of as a "love letter" to the family. Ethical wills have their roots in the Old Testament and were originally transmitted orally. Over time, ethical wills have become more formalized, and today usually take written form. With today's technology, many people use a video camera to record their message for future generations, and some have even created websites for this purpose. Every ethical will is unique and is based upon the writer's own life story. However, there are certain characteristics common to most ethical wills. Typically, an ethical will would contain the writer's beliefs and values system; spiritual values; hopes and blessings for future generations; declarations of love; life lessons; and declarations of forgiveness and requests for forgiveness from others.

Given their obvious appeal, why have ethical wills been so frequently ignored? There are many reasons, but the primary roadblock is that it is difficult for people to put their thoughts and feelings into words. Even those people who love the concept will often become stymied as they stare at that blank piece of paper; how does one express their most heartfelt feelings and values—to tell their life's story?

Consulting with an attorney or other professional advisor who focuses on the non-financial aspects of legacy planning can help you get on your way. Another great resource is *celebrationsoflife.net*, where you can find many resources for preparing an ethical will, including many sample ethical wills from people at different stages of life.

While the effective design and implementation of an estate plan will serve to pass financial resources—real property, investments, and personal items—to children, grandchildren or other loved ones, using estate planning tools to pass values and to help develop character is often a more important concern for people planning their estates. That's where incentive planning comes in.

Parents use both incentives and disincentives to shape character and conduct during life, and they can continue to do so after they are gone. Having made careful choices with their finances, and having used their wealth to benefit others, clients rarely want to see that wealth squandered by their heirs. Incentive planning allows people to continue to positively influence later generations.

Incentive planning is not for everyone. Some see it as "controlling from the grave." But once exposed to the concept, many clients choose to include some measure of incentive planning in their estate plans.

For some families, education is the top priority. Common education incentives may include (but are certainly not limited to):

- Paying for a child or grandchild's enrollment in private or parochial school
- Establishing a college fund to assist a child or grandchild to attend the most challenging college that accepts him or her
- Permitting discretionary funds to be made available only if the child or grandchild maintains a certain grade point average
- Paying a bonus upon graduation

For other families, encouraging productive work is a top priority. A plan may provide for matching funds for savings accounts built through after school or summer jobs. Or the plan may establish a pool of resources to fund business ventures or a professional practice. Other people may want to encourage a particular career-choice that follows a family tradition. An incentive might be offered to a child who foregoes monetary rewards by becoming a teacher, social worker or entering the ministry. For example, the plan may match the income sacrificed by the child in honoring the values of the parent. Such a plan serves as a form of "internal" family philanthropy, with "grants" of support based on clearly delineated criteria rather than strict equality amongst all the children or other beneficiaries.

Incentive planning is an exciting topic to explore. The options are limited only by the creativity of the client and their professional advisors.

Chapter 24 - Counseling: The Key To An Effective Estate Plan

A consistent theme throughout this book has been the importance of utilizing a counseling-based estate planning approach to achieve the best results. Through real-world examples, I have demonstrated the results that effective counseling-based estate planning can achieve. Equally instructive, this book contains numerous examples of estate planning "gone wrong," with usually the cause being (i) insufficient or ineffective counseling regarding the planning options available for the circumstances, or (ii) the failure of the affected party to seek legal counsel to address the issue.

A skilled estate planning and elder law attorney has numerous tools in his or her estate planning "toolbox" to achieve the desired outcome. But having the tools is not enough, as do-it-yourself legal software can provide virtually any person with similar if not identical tools. What an experienced and knowledgeable estate planning attorney offers, however, is the unique training and experience to analyze the client's personal situation and develop a comprehensive planning strategy custom-tailored to that client's needs and objectives. Only after the plan is properly designed will the appropriate legal tools be utilized to bring the plan to life.

Some, but by no means all, factors to be evaluated in analyzing a particular case include:

- The age and health of the client(s)
- The client's financial picture, including the client's income, type of assets owned and title of ownership
- The possible need for and likely effectiveness of proactive long-term care planning, including the use of a MAPT
- The family structure and relationships, including:

- Single marriage vs. blended family
- Family harmony or disharmony
- Children or grandchildren with special needs
- The financial outlook of the children or other potential beneficiaries

- Whether the client is philanthropic
- Whether real estate is owned in multiple jurisdictions
- Pending or proposed changes in the legal landscape -- new tax laws, Medicaid laws, laws affecting creditor and debtor rights, etc.
- The nature and effectiveness of any existing estate planning

As in any profession, not all attorneys are created equal, and finding the right attorney for your estate planning and elder law needs requires some due diligence. There are many excellent attorneys, but your estate planning and elder law needs require the attention of an attorney who concentrates in those practice areas. So, where might you begin your search? One option is to ask friends and family if they have experience with a counseling-oriented estate planning attorney. Another option is to contact your local or state Bar Associations for a referral to an estate planning and/or elder law attorney in your vicinity.

For elder law matters, a Certified Elder Law Attorney (CELA) designation provides assurance that the attorney has the highest credentials available to an elder law attorney. CELAs must pass a difficult exam and must devote a substantial amount of their professional time handling elder law matters.

Another resource is the *National Association of Estate Planners & Councils* (naepc.org), which is an umbrella organization comprising attorneys, financial advisors, accountants, and insurance professionals who work in estate planning; there are approximately 260 local councils throughout the United States where you can find local estate planning attorneys. But perhaps the best resource for finding an outstanding estate planning and elder law attorney is to contact one or more of the national organizations that provide support and services to estate planning and elder law attorneys, including *Wealthcounsel* (wealthcounsel.com), *Eldercounsel (*eldercounsel.com), *Elderlawanswers* (elderlawansers.com), *National Network of Estate Planning Attorneys (nnepa.com),* and *National Academy of Elder Law Attorneys* (naela.org).

Whichever route you take to find a counseling-based estate planning and elder attorney, I urge you to act NOW, as being proactive will almost always lead to a more favorable result than being reactive. As aptly noted by one of the world's creative geniuses:

> *Only put off until tomorrow what you are willing to die having left undone*
>
> – Pablo Picasso

Appendix A

2022 Community Spouse Medicaid Allowances

State	Community Spouse Resource Allowance (CSRA)		Monthly Maintenance Needs Allowance (MMMNA)	
	Minimum	Maximum	Minimum	Maximum
AL	$27,480.00	$137,400.00	$2,177.50	$2,177.50
AK	$137,400.00	$137,400.00	$3,435.00	$3,435.00
AZ	$27,480.00	$137,400.00	$2,177.50	$3,535.00
AR	$27,480.00	$137,400.00	$2,177.50	$3,435.00
CA	$137,400.00	$137,400.00	$3,435.00	$3,435.00
CO	$27,480.00	$137,400.00	$2,177.50	$3,435.00
CT	$27,480.00	$137,400.00	$2,177.50	$3,435.00
DC	$27,480.00	$137,400.00	$2,177.50	$2,177.50
DE	$27,480.00	$137,400.00	$2,177.50	$3,435.00
FL	$137,400.00	$137,400.00	$2,177.50	$3,535.00
GA	$137,400.00	$137,400.00	$3,435.00	$3,435.00
HI	$137,400.00	$137,400.00	$2,505.00	$3,435.00
ID	$27,480.00	$137,400.00	$2,177.50	$3,435.00
IL	$109,560.00	$109,560.00	$2,739.00	$2,739.00
IN	$27,480.00	$137,400.00	$2,177.50	$3,435.00
IA	$27,480.00	$137,400.00	$3,435.00	$3,535.00
KS	$27,480.00	$137,400.00	$2,177.50	$3,435.00

KY	$27,480.00	$137,400.00	$2,177.50	$3,435.00
LA	$137,400.00	$137,400.00	$3,435.00	$3,435.00
ME	$137,400.00	$137,400.00	$2,177.50	$3,435.00
MD	$27,480.00	$137,400.00	$2,177.50	$3,435.00
MA	$137,400.00	$137,400.00	$2,177.50	$3,435.00
MI	$27,480.00	$137,400.00	$2,177.50	$3,535.00
MN	$137,400.00	$137,400.00	$2,177.50	$3,435.00
MS	$137,400.00	$137,400.00	$3,435.00	$3,435.00
MO	$27,480.00	$137,400.00	$2,177.50	$3,435.00
MT	$27,480.00	$137,400.00	$2,177.50	$3,435.00
NE	$27,480.00	$137,400.00	$2,177.50	$3,435.00
NV	$27,480.00	$137,400.00	$2,177.50	$3,435.00
NH	$27,480.00	$137,400.00	$2,177.50	$3,435.00
NJ	$27,480.00	$137,400.00	$2,177.50	$3,435.00
NM	$31,290.00	$137,400.00	$2,177.50	$3,435.00
NY	$74,820.00	$137,400.00	$3,425.00	$3,435.00
NC	$27,480.00	$137,400.00	$2,177.50	$3,435.00
ND	$27,480.00	$137,400.00	$3,435.00	$3,435.00
OH	$27,480.00	$137,400.00	$2,177.50	$3,435.00
OK	$27,480.00	$137,400.00	$3,435.00	$3,435.00
OR	$27,480.00	$137,400.00	$2,177.50	$3,435.00
PA	$27,480.00	$137,400.00	$2,177.50	$3,435.00

RI	$27,480.00	$137,400.00	$2,177.50	$3,435.00
SC	$66,480.00	$66,480.00	$3,435.00	$3,435.00
SD	$27,480.00	$137,400.00	$2,177.50	$3,435.00
TN	$27,480.00	$137,400.00	$2,177.50	$3,435.00
TX	$27,480.00	$137,400.00	$3,435.00	$3,435.00
UT	$27,480.00	$137,400.00	$2,177.50	$3,435.00
VT	$137,400.00	$137,400.00	$2,177.50	$3,435.00
VA	$27,480.00	$137,400.00	$2,177.50	$3,435.00
WA	$59,890.00	$137,400.00	$2,177.50	$3,435.00
WV	$27,480.00	$137,400.00	$2,177.50	$3,435.00
WI	$50,000.00	$137,400.00	$2,903.34	$3,435.00
WY	$137,400.00	$137,400.00	$3,435.00	$3,435.00

INDEX

529 plans, 98, 100, 101
ACA, 172
advance directives, 20
Affordable Care Act, 172
annual exclusion, 30, 31, 96, 98
annuity, 164, 184, 185, 188, 203
applicable federal rate, 158
applicable resource allowance, 152
Assisted Living Residence, 146, 147
available resource, 43, 59, 75, 106, 158, 167, 185
Blended Families, 58
bloodline protection, 19, 211
capital gains tax, 16, 70, 85, 97, 128, 131, 155, 187, 189, 197, 211
Centers for Medicare & Medicaid Services, 144
charitable deduction, 188, 190, 191
Charitable Gift Annuities, 188
Charitable Lead Trust, 189
charitable planning, 191
Charitable Remainder Trust, 79, 188
CLT, 189
Community Medicaid, 6, 7, 140, 141, 142, 144, 145, 147, 148, 171
Community Spouse, 162, 163, 164, 165, 166, 185, 221
Community Spouse Resource Allowance, 162, 221
Continuing Care Retirement Community, 145
countable resources, 125, 129, 140, 143, 150, 164, 170, 171, 175, 176, 182, 184
COVID-19, 142, 144, 195
Crisis Medicaid, 183
Deficit Reduction Act, 148, 154, 159
Department of Social Services, 139, 150, 161, 163, 166, 169, 170, 173, 176
disabled beneficiaries, 63, 79, 143, 172
disabled person, 63, 64, 65, 66, 153, 166, 172, 173
donee, 96, 97, 100
durable power of attorney, 12, 120, 130, 184
Dynasty Trusts, 104
Education Savings Plans, 98
Elder Law, i, 21, 55, 145, 219, 220
eligibility threshold, 150
Enhanced Assisted Living Residence, 147

equity exemption, 151
Estate Plan Maintenance, 54
estate tax exemption, 15, 25, 31, 84, 86, 90, 91, 92, 93, 94, 103, 193, 195, 196, 206, 213
estate tax protection, 104, 107
estate taxes, 31, 73, 84, 85, 90, 93, 103, 104, 189, 192, 195, 206, 213
executor, 9, 29, 38, 68, 86, 90, 92, 206, 207
exempt transfer, 125, 143, 144, 149, 152, 153, 157
Family Home Exemption, 151
family trust, 15, 16, 25, 84
FDIC, 45, 46, 47, 48
gift tax exemption, iv, 30, 64, 90, 96, 100, 196, 214
gift tax liability, 86, 195
Grantor Retained Annuity Trust, 159
guardian ad litem, 5
Half-a-Loaf, 156
health care powers of attorney, 20
HIPAA Authorizations, 20
ILIT, 103, 104
inheritance taxes, 93
intestate, 4, 6, 8
IRA, 50, 73, 75, 76, 77, 78, 79, 167, 168
irrevocable life insurance trust, 32
irrevocable trust, 17, 19, 36, 53, 113, 126, 129, 130, 159, 195, 198, 201, 211
last will and testament, 2, 119
life estate, 130, 131, 132, 154, 155
Life Insurance, 103, 104, 106, 107, 109, 188, 214
life insurance policy, 31, 50, 62, 71, 103, 104, 106, 108, 109, 111
Life Settlement, 107, 108, 109
lifetime exemption, 96
lifetime gifts, 36, 87, 88, 114, 199
lifetime protective trust, 16, 49, 59, 210, 211
limited liability company, 55, 83
LLC, 83, 84, 88, 113, 177, 202
long-term care, 2, 6, 13, 17, 19, 21, 22, 35, 40, 43, 50, 52, 55, 59, 69, 75, 97, 104, 105, 106, 112, 121, 123, 125, 126, 127, 130, 131, 133, 134, 135, 136, 138, 139, 140, 143, 144, 148, 151, 159, 160, 162, 171, 172, 183, 185, 195, 218

Long-term care insurance, 146
look-back, 59, 125, 127, 132, 140, 143, 144, 145, 147, 148, 149, 152, 156, 161, 168, 169, 171, 172, 174, 175, 176, 177, 180
MAPR, 181, 182
MAPT, 125, 126, 127, 128, 129, 130, 131, 132, 172, 211, 218
marital agreements, 86, 88
marital deduction, 25, 67, 192
maximum benefit, 156
Medicaid application, 139, 142, 143, 148, 150, 151, 152, 153, 160, 165, 170, 174, 176
Medicaid approval, 164, 175
Medicaid Asset Protection, 7, 52, 59, 68, 125, 172, 180, 211
Medicaid Asset Protection Trusts, 59, 211
Medicaid benefits, 17, 64, 140, 144, 151, 159, 185
Medicaid determination, 175, 176
Medicaid eligibility, 6, 7, 23, 35, 64, 66, 69, 97, 138, 139, 147, 148, 151, 152, 164, 165, 166, 168, 173, 175, 176, 179
Medicaid GRAT, 159
Medicaid ineligibility, 125, 150, 152, 158, 160
Medicaid penalty, 149, 150, 152, 154, 160, 162, 169, 177
Medicaid planning, 17, 30, 69, 97, 121, 127, 176, 181, 198
Minimum Monthly Maintenance Needs Allowance, 162
Non-Citizen Spouse, 84
nonexempt asset transfers, 148, 156
non-exempt assets, 156
not-for-profit, 171
Nursing Home, 147, 152, 176
Nursing Home Care, 147
Outright gifts, 187
penalty period, 143, 144, 145, 149, 150, 156, 157, 158, 160, 161, 162, 168, 169, 171, 174, 175, 176, 177, 182, 183
Pooled Income Trust, 141, 142, 172
Portability, 21, 91
prenuptial agreement, 19, 43, 50
Probate, 8, 14
promissory note, 34, 72, 157, 158, 159, 185

QDOT, 85, 86
QPRT, 195, 196, 197
QTIP, 88, 192, 193
Qualified Domestic Trust, 85
qualified terminable interest property, 192
Regional Rate, 143, 144, 149, 157, 161
retirement accounts, 69, 74, 76, 77, 80, 149, 166, 167, 168
revocable living trust, 14, 46, 47, 49, 51, 68, 192
RLT, 14, 15, 16
Roth IRA, 73, 76, 168
Santa Clause, 95
SECURE Act, iv, 74, 77, 78, 79
SNT, 17, 43, 62, 63, 170, 171, 172, 173
Social Security, 6, 67, 139, 141, 152, 156, 157, 168, 184, 185
special needs, 14, 21, 61, 62, 63, 219
Special Needs Irrevocable Life Insurance Trust, 106
spend down, 18, 19, 30, 125, 141, 163, 167, 180, 184, 209
Split-Interest Gift Trust, 188
spousal refusal, 69, 145, 156, 163, 184
spousal right of election, 10, 43
SSI, 61, 62, 64, 65, 66, 170, 171
statutory exception, 161
STOLI, 109, 110, 111
Supplemental Needs Trust, 43, 61, 66, 153
survivorship, 9, 10, 11, 37, 50, 92, 112, 183
Tax Cut and Jobs Act, 190
Tax Relief, 90, 91
taxable estate, 49, 74, 86, 94, 96, 100, 103, 104, 107, 114, 189, 192, 193, 195, 196, 197, 199, 211
tenants by the entirety, 112
trustmaker, 14, 15, 17, 19, 52, 82, 114, 119, 120, 124, 126, 127, 128, 129, 198, 211
under hardship, 169
undue influence, 44
Unlimited Marital Deduction, 85, 86
VA, 181, 182
vacation home, 54, 82, 83, 84, 195
vacation home trust, 83, 84
Veterans Aid and Attendance, 181
well spouse, 156, 164
windfall, 100, 170, 171, 172

225

www.ingramcontent.com/pod-product-compliance
Lightning Source LLC
LaVergne TN
LVHW021811060526
838201LV00058B/3323